Sybil MacBeth

The
Season
of the Nativity

Confessions and Practices of an Advent,
Christmas & Epiphany Extremist

PARACLETE PRESS
BREWSTER, MASSACHUSETTS

· · · · · · · · · · For Andy,
my longtime, cherished partner
in the daily liturgy of life and love.

2 0 1 4
First printing *The*
Season of the Nativity: Confessions and
Practices of an Advent, Christmas, and Epiphany
Extremist Copyright © 2014 by Sybil MacBeth ISBN
978-1-61261-410-6 Unless otherwise marked, Scripture
references are taken from the New Revised Standard Version
Bible, copyright 1989, Division of Christian Education of the National
Council of the Churches of Christ in the United States of America. Used
by permission. All rights reserved. Scriptures marked (NIV) are taken
from THE HOLY BIBLE, NEW INTERNATIONAL VERSION®, NIV®
Copyright © 1973, 1978, 1984, 2011 by Biblica, Inc.® Used by permission.
All rights reserved worldwide. Scriptures marked (KJV) are taken from the
Authorized King James Version of the Holy Bible. The Paraclete Press
name and logo (dove on cross) are trademarks of Paraclete Press, Inc.
All rights reserved. No portion of this book may be reproduced, stored
in an electronic retrieval system, or transmitted in any form or by
any means—electronic, mechanical, photocopy, recording, or
any other—except for brief quotations in printed reviews,
without the prior permission of the publisher. Published
by Paraclete Press Brewster, Massachusetts
www.paracletepress.com Printed in the
United States of America

10 9 8 7 6 5 4 3 2 1

Library of Congress Cataloging-in-Publication Data
MacBeth, Sybil.
    The season of the Nativity : confessions and practices of an Advent, Christmas, and
Epiphany extremist / Sybil MacBeth.
        pages cm
    Includes bibliographical references.
    ISBN 978-1-61261-410-6 (pb with french flaps)
    1. Jesus Christ—Nativity—Miscellanea. 2. Advent—Miscellanea. 3. Christmas—
Miscellanea. 4. Epiphany season—Miscellanea. 5. Church year--Miscellanea.
6. MacBeth, Sybil. I. Title.
    BV45.M324 2014
    263'.91—dc23   2014020145

Contents

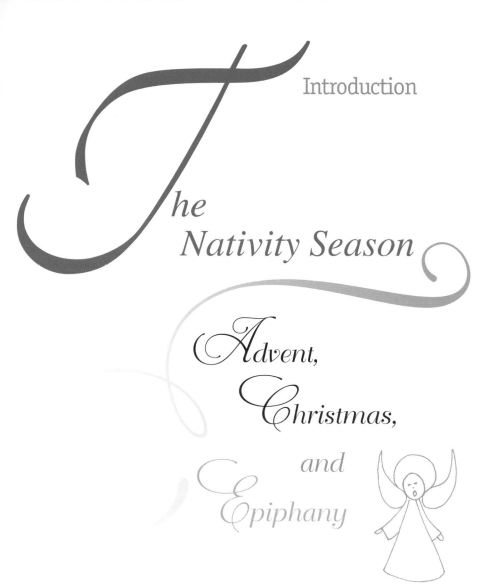

The Nativity Season

Advent, Christmas, and Epiphany

Here is a skeleton snapshot of the Nativity season. Throughout this book more flesh, muscle, and sinews will be added to these bare-bones definitions of Advent, Christmas, and Epiphany.

Advent recounts and remembers the **events prior to Jesus's birth.** For more than a thousand years, the ancient peoples who became the Israelites longed for a Savior. They wanted freedom from slavery and captivity. Abraham, Sarah, Moses, Isaac, Rachel, and a host of other spiritual relatives trusted the One God to listen to their cries and send a Messiah who would rescue them. Advent recalls their longings, their dreams, and their waiting for the One who would free them. The Scripture readings, the themes, and the songs of this season are full of the promises, prophecies, and predictions of the Savior and Liberator whom God will send.

Christmas celebrates **the birth of Jesus.** Christmas is the fulfillment of Advent waiting. This is the time for rejoicing and Alleluias. God has given the world an unexpected Savior, born in a small town in a small stable or cave to people with no worldly status. Peace will come.

Epiphany heralds the **ramifications of Jesus's birth.** The arrival of the Magi from foreign lands foretells the day when faraway people will learn about this surprising Savior. Jesus cannot be contained in his own land with just his own people. His saving work will go viral and spread to the ends of the earth.

C onfessions

I t's five in the evening. An almost-winter sunset of fuchsia, salmon, and hot pink paints its way above the rooflines in my Memphis neighborhood. It's so beautiful I gasp. I grasp for words to describe what I see: cotton candy, tie-dyed T-shirts, cooked shrimp. Words fail, turning the magnificent into verbal mush.

In just a matter of minutes the scene changes: the sun descends and the colors morph from reddish, pinkish hues to gray and midnight blue. Darkness comes fast now. And as if directed by a tuxedo-dressed conductor standing in the middle of our street, hundreds of tiny lights pop on with the rhythmic energy of a Brandenburg Concerto. Back and forth across the street, red, green, and white lights burst forth to highlight trees, eaves, and doorways. Santa appears on the right side, reindeers on the left; penguins on the right, snowmen on the left. It's a symphony of light and color. It's spectacular and magical—an amusement park light show right in my neighbors' front yards. The darkness is aglow with Christmas celebration. I am at once delighted, then horrified. Good grief, it is only November 15—a full six weeks before Christmas.

I have sometimes hated Christmas. For the first twenty years of my adulthood, I tried to create the perfect Christmas. I roamed malls and overbaked and sent Christmas cards and threw in some spiritual reading here and there. By the time December 25 rolled around I was tired, irritable, and needed to make amends to everyone in the radius of my voice. My not very successful, excessive gift purchases and the twenty-three kinds of cookies from my Christmas bake-off turned my stomach. Nobody really wanted the items I had chosen to clutter their house and closets; nobody wanted all of the sugar and butter I had baked to cling to their arteries and thighs. I've toned down the gift giving and the culinary prep a bit, but the temptation to host a magazine-worthy Christmas still looms and lures. If the previous sentences make you think "What a Scrooge!" and "Bah! Humbug! lady," please bear in mind, I only *partly* hate Christmas.

I also *love* Christmas. Christmas, in my opinion, gets short shrift. For some reason, Christians have made the death, atonement, and resurrection of the Easter season the most important focus of theology and worship. We seem to have forgotten the mystery and wonder of Jesus's mere existence and life on earth. The concept of the Incarnation—God coming to "dwell among us" as flesh and blood—is so fanciful and so reckless, it deserves more attention. Christmas heralds Jesus's birth and therefore needs better PR and better coverage as a spiritual celebration. It is not just the lightweight cousin of Easter.

What I *really* love is the parentheses of weeks on either side of Christmas called Advent and Epiphany. Advent rolls out the red carpet in anticipation of Jesus's birth. Epiphany extends the carpet into the future beyond his birth and birthplace. The whole Nativity Season deserves to be relished. The Nativity of Jesus includes the three seasons of Advent, Christmas, and Epiphany. These seasons form a triptych—a three-part picture of the events surrounding the birth of Jesus. I want people to luxuriate in the forty-plus days called Advent, Christmas, and Epiphany: Let Advent start four Sundays before Christmas and last until the night of December 24. Celebrate Christmas from December 25 until January 5—all Twelve Days. Gather on January 6 Eve for the start of Epiphany and let it linger until, well, maybe even, Lent.

The first part of the Nativity triptych, Advent, is my favorite season of the year. The darkness and cold of impending winter set the stage for the four weeks of preparation before Christmas. If people have a home season, mine is winter. As the days shorten and the sunsets grow more colorful and more ominous, my mood becomes pensive and dark. Advent invites me to hunker down and nestle in. It encourages me to go indoors and inward. I love the waiting and the anticipation. During Advent, Mary is pregnant with the Christ child; I am pregnant with longing and hope for a new way to know God.

I call myself an Advent Extremist. Other people call me an Advent Fundamentalist or Advent Militant. "Get on with the holidays, the merriment, the celebration," people sometimes say. "Why the doom and gloom, the seriousness?" "Advent *is* serious," I say. But for me, it is also full of delight. Advent is both work and play. Without the work and the preparation, there are no fireworks and no real party at Christmas, just a high and a letdown. Without Advent, the celebration of Christmas feels a bit empty.

I also love this time of year for another reason. The Nativity season gives me permission to be—do I dare say the *r*-word?—*Religious. Religious* has gotten a bad reputation in the past hundred years. It has come to mean pious, self-righteous, holding mindless belief, and practicing empty ritual. Although I am tempted at times to describe myself as "spiritual but not religious"—because *spiritual* feels freer, less judgmental, more in touch with the Divine, and more loving—I have a deep *religious* sensibility. I want to be both spiritual *and* religious.

Religious means having an outward way to make visible inner feelings like gratitude, awe, and sorrow.

I need a way to articulate and incarnate the spiritual thoughts, questions, and beliefs that flutter around my mind. Grateful, awestruck, and sorry need a framework for their expression. Practices and rituals are important to me because they give form to my devotion and evolving belief and provide a structure for worship and study. During this Nativity season, my non-Christian friends and my "spiritual but not religious" friends give me a break. They let me wax *religious* without apology. They don't give me a hard time. I think they secretly like my Advent calendars, my cracked and peeling porcelain Nativity set, and my Epiphany bush.

For two and a half decades Advent was the main focus of my Nativity season attention. As an Advent Extremist, I lavished hours of time on keeping a Holy Advent. The weeks of home-front rituals, quiet reflection time, and the display of the liturgical symbols and colors of Advent were my idea of a good time. After Advent, I dropped the ball. Except for the single days of December 25 and January 6, I mostly ignored Christmas and Epiphany as seasons. But in recent years, Christmas and Epiphany have clamored for their due. Their pleas for recognition and respect are justified; they deserve a shelf life of more than one day. To make up for my past neglect I have explored old traditions and initiated fresh rituals to celebrate and honor their distinctive roles in the Nativity season. Every year I become a bigger and bigger advocate—maybe even an Extremist—of their extended life span.

easons to Read This Book

Here are some reasons you might want to read this book:

✳ **You swore last Christmas** that next year would be different. You would pay more attention to Jesus and less attention to creating a perfect Christmas.

✳ **You've heard the words** *Advent* and *Epiphany* but don't really know what they are all about.

✳ **You want to create rituals** and traditions that teach your children about Jesus and the stories of the season.

✳ **You want to avoid the big rush** to Christmas, and the huge letdown when the packages have been opened and the Christmas dinner eaten.

✳ **You have little time** for reflection and meditation but want to do something to prepare spiritually for Christmas.

※ **You are fidgety,** distractible, and word-weary. You want some non-reading ways to participate in Advent.

※ **You don't want to dread** the holidays.

※ **You want some ways** to experience the spirituality of the holiday season as a family.

※ **You want to feel less chaos** and more serenity.

※ **You love Christmas** but you are often "over it" well before December 25.

※ **You grew up as a Christian** but with little emphasis on the spiritual practices and rituals. You would like to expand your repertoire of ways to focus on the religious/spiritual aspects of the holidays.

※ **You are a serious Christian** looking for new ways to celebrate the Nativity season.

※ **You have little free time** in your schedule and want some simple, quick Advent, Christmas, and Epiphany activities.

※ **You have doubts** about Wise Men coming to a manger and shepherds in fields, but you are still interested in how those stories might point to something larger about Jesus and God.

※ **You want to decorate** your Christmas tree on November 15 but you also want to incorporate some of the Advent ideas of watching and waiting.

※ **You are looking for things to do** after December 25, other than just sing "The Twelve Days of Christmas."

※ **You want exercises** and ideas for creating personal discipline this season.

※ **You think of yourself as "spiritual but not religious,"** but would like to understand what the Christian/Christmas story might add to your spiritual life.

My Calendars

Here is another confession. I love games. If someone offered me a salary to play Scrabble® and Sudoku all day long, the temptation would be too great to resist. Unscrambling letters and organizing numbers is my idea of a tasty cerebral feast.

I love all kinds of games: card games, board games, word games, math games, team games, solo games, athletic games. . . . The list is long. From my childhood I remember two frequent, regular activities in our house: prayers and games. My mother prayed with me; my father taught me board games. With Candy Land®, my father initiated me into a lifelong fascination with luck and strategy.

I loved the Candy Land® board with its colorful switchback trail through the Candy Cane Forest and into the Gumdrop Mountains. From start to finish, it wound back and forth from the bottom to the top in a ribbon of red, yellow, green, orange, purple, and pink rectangles. Each player drew a card, usually saw one or two rectangles of a particular color and advanced their pawn along the path to the Candy Castle to either the first or second rectangle of the chosen color.

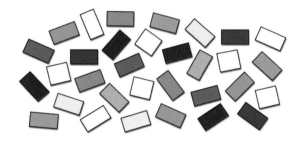

From Candy Land®, I graduated to Sorry!® and Parcheesi®. Sorry!® required more thought and skill than Candy Land®. Using a deck of cards with instructions, players on the Sorry!® board moved their red, blue, yellow, or green playing pieces on a path of white rectangles around the edge of the board. The winner successfully moved all four of his or her pieces from Start to Home before the other players. Parcheesi®, also a board game, similar to Sorry!® had a pathway of rectangles around the board in the shape of a cross. On the high shelf of the coat closet in our living room, board games tottered in precarious piles. These games taught me to count, to strategize, to win and lose, to wait my turn, and to play in community.

I also attribute my understanding of time to my early exposure to board games. All of my early childhood games had rectangles. When I first learned the days of the week I imagined them as rectangles on an oval. Monday, Tuesday, Wednesday, and Thursday were located on the right side of the oval; Friday was at the top. Saturday and Sunday filled up the entire left side—my early learning about the importance of weekends! I tracked the days of my childhood by imagining myself traipsing counterclockwise week after week around the oval on rectangular stepping-stones.

Maybe this oval was just childish imagination, but this visual calendar is still my mental weekly events' planner. If it's Monday and I'm thinking about dinner with friends on Friday, I walk four spaces in my head to Friday, toddle uphill to noon, cross into the bright hours of afternoon, and go downhill to the darkening hours of dusk until I land on the seven o'clock spot. If I'm thinking about an appointment on Saturday from Monday's vantage point, I might just peer across the oval. Board games, it seems, gave me a way to *visualize* the passage of time.

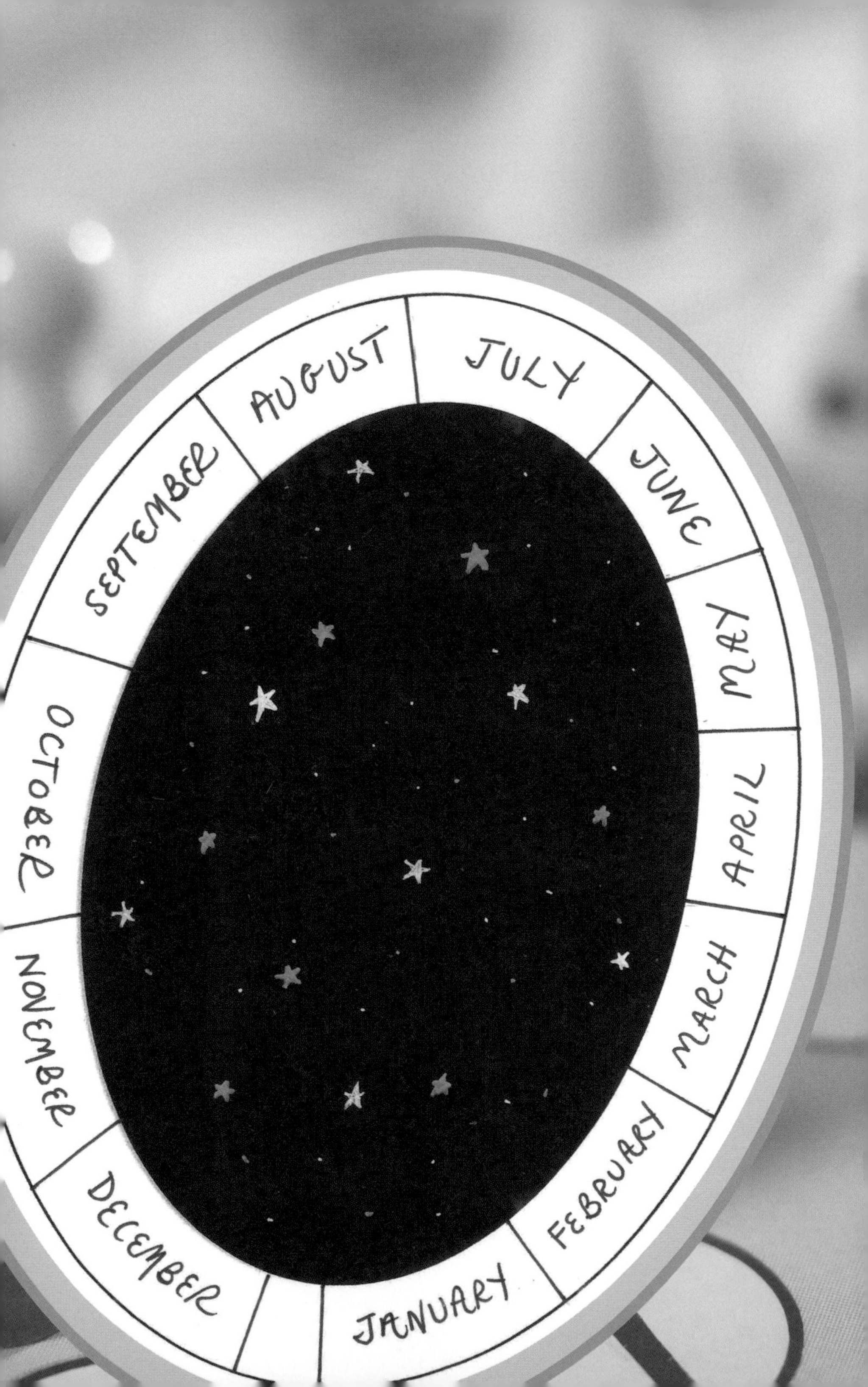
JULY
AUGUST
SEPTEMBER
OCTOBER
NOVEMBER
DECEMBER
JANUARY
FEBRUARY
MARCH
APRIL
MAY
JUNE

In my visual universe, the *year* is also an oval with rectangles for the months. December and January are at the bottom, February through May are on the right side. June, July, and August swing around the top: September, October, and November are on the left side. Inside the months are rectangles equal to the number of days. There is a little gap between December and January. The rectangles on the oval are not a single color like the Candy Land® game but are filled with colorful images of the people and events planned for those days and months. There is a little home movie playing on every day of the year. And did I mention: the ellipse floats in the starlit blackness of the solar system?

If you think this is just a little crazy, you might be right. But as a visual construct, the oval created a framework for me to understand the forward movement of my life within a repeating cycle of days, weeks, months, and years.

Chapter 4

The Liturgical Calendar

The first time I heard the phrase "liturgical year" was probably during a confirmation class I attended at age twenty. I was about to marry my Episcopal boyfriend, who wanted to make sure I was part of *his* church family before our marriage. I doubt I actually heard the "liturgical year" phrase during the class; I was too busy wondering if I could reconcile the metaphysical and perfection-oriented teachings of my Christian Science background with the down and dirty, orthodox Christian theology of my fiancé's church. Christian Science proclaimed God's creation and creatures as free from sin, sickness, evil, and death. Episcopalians professed out loud, "There is no health in us," and confessed their sinfulness in public. Similar to the way I was born two decades before—feet first—I came kicking and squawking into this new church. The concept of a liturgical year and a liturgical calendar was the least of the seismic shifts in my spiritual psyche.

The church of my childhood paid little attention to Christmas and Easter as days of celebration. In Sunday school we learned about the birth of Jesus, his life, his performance of healings and miracles, and his resurrection. There were no Christmas or Easter services. The only indications of either holiday in the church building were an occasional poinsettia in December and the brand new spring hats, outfits, and corsages worn by female members on Easter Sunday.

I learned the meaning of the word *liturgy* in the Episcopal Church. *Liturgy* means "the work of the people." It is the words, actions, and participation of the Christian community in response to God's presence in the world. The response comes in the forms and rituals of communal worship as well as in the personal practices of Christians at home and in the world.

Over hundreds of years, the church created a calendar of feast days, Sundays, and seasons that emphasize key events in the life and ministry of Jesus and honor important people in the Christian story (both biblical and post-biblical characters). The appointed Scripture readings (or lectionary), prayers, hymns, and environment reflect the themes and theology of each season. Catholics, Lutherans, Anglicans, Orthodox, and other Christian denominations use a liturgical calendar to frame worship and study. Together these days and seasons form "the church year," or "the liturgical year."

Some of the dates of the liturgical seasons vary according to a lunar calendar; some vary in relationship to fixed dates, like Christmas, which is always December 25. With some variation among denominations and traditions, the liturgical or church year of Western Christianity is divided into the following main seasons:

Ordinary Time
Pentecost to Advent

Ordinary Time focuses on the ministry, teaching, preaching, parables, and miracles of Jesus. It is the time Christians put their faith into practice rather than just prepare for and celebrate its high points of Christmas and Easter.

Color: Green

Advent
starts with the first of four Sundays before Christmas.

This is the Sunday nearest November 30. Advent lasts until the first worship service of Christmas on Christmas Eve.

Colors: Purple or blue

Christmas
December 25 to January 5

Color: White

Epiphany
January 6 to Lent

Officially the period from January 7 until Lent is called Ordinary Time, but I think Epiphany deserves more than just one day of attention.

Color: White (or green if considered Ordinary Time)

entecost

celebrates the day when Jesus's disciples and followers received the gift of the Holy Spirit. This day is often called the Birthday of the Church.

Color: Red

aster

Easter Day (date varies with lunar calendar)

celebrates the resurrection of Jesus and lasts fifty days until the Day of Pentecost.

Color: White

ent

is the 40 days (excluding Sundays) before Easter, starting with Ash Wednesday.

Lent is a season of reflection and penitence in preparation for Easter. Palm Sunday and Holy Week recount the events of the last week of Jesus's life and the Crucifixion.

Colors: Purple/violet or off-white; red for Palm Sunday and Holy Week

Since I was new to the liturgical tradition, it took me years to understand the patterns and cycle of the yearly celebrations. It also took several years for me to acclimate to the rituals and ceremony of worship. The gestures, stained glass, crosses, candles, fancy vestments on the clergy/lay presiders, and colors associated with the seasons seemed a little bit hocus-pocus. The attention paid to these physical, aesthetic details was foreign and even contrary to the unadorned, sensory-free worship of my childhood.

This was Planet Episcopal, and I was an alien. I was used to WORDS—words in readings and hymns—but with no visual or physical aesthetics to distract from them. My first months in this new church felt like an assault. How can you pay attention to the WORDS with all of these distractions? Wasn't all of this sensory stimulation and attention to the visual a form of idolatry? Weren't these seasons sort of arbitrary and confining?

In about year five in my life on the new planet—still struggling with creeds and theology—I began to appreciate the rhythm, the reason, the wisdom, and the joy of liturgical worship and practice. The calendar was a way to guide me through the Scriptures in a three-year cycle. It was both a teaching and a worship tool. The liturgical year became a kind of syllabus for learning the Christian narrative: Jesus's conception, birth, life, teaching, preaching, troublemaking, rabblerousing, healings, miracles, arrest, death, and resurrection. The logic and order of the calendar appealed to my mathematical brain. At the same time, the connections of the calendar, the stories and the embodied, sensory experience on Sunday morning moved my worship, belief, and practice from my head to my heart and then to my whole person.

If my mind wandered during the readings or the sermon and I lost track of the words, the story was still within "eyeshot." I was surrounded by all kinds of sensory and physical stimuli to pull me back into the moment. The stained-glass windows told me stories with pictures; the candles symbolized Christ's light and the way through the darkness; the smell of the sometimes-used incense dizzied me with the mystery of God; the soaring architecture celebrated the grandeur of God; the music vibrated through my skin and bones; the colors filled my eyes with the theological themes of the season. Sometimes given a bad reputation by ill-informed people, such as I was, these physical embellishments were not extraneous; they catered to people with differing learning styles and different attention spans. This was not idolatry, as I had thought; it was an invitation to bring my whole body and personality to worship.

The liturgical year, or calendar, with its corresponding stories and practices adds another layer to my understanding of life and time. Superimposed onto my childhood oval of rectangles, it is a transparency on top of my "regular" calendar. The two calendars merge and blur the lines between my secular and sacred life. My own small life, embedded in a spiritual calendar, weaves its way into the Big story of God and God's ongoing work in the world. My calendars are the picture of my life as a Christian where God is the centerfold of all of my appointments and events. Together, my regular calendar and the liturgical calendar provide a framework for ordering and chronicling my life.

The liturgical calendar with its seasons of Advent, Christmas, Epiphany, Lent, Easter, Pentecost, and Ordinary Time adds a new spiritual dimension to my life. My trek around the oval is not just a yearly journey; it is a pilgrimage. I am not walking alone or just with people from my own time; the biblical characters and my spiritual ancestors accompany me along the way.

Year after year an annual family reunion happens. We retell the family stories and chronicle the story of God's presence in the world. This repeated cycle of stories and celebrations is not just a stagnant repetition or instant replay of previous years. Every year I am different from who I was 365 days ago, and I see my ancestors and history with fresh eyes. The experiences of the past twelve months affect my vision. New friends and a growing extended family provide different filters. Career changes and moves to a different state change my physical geography. I read new books.

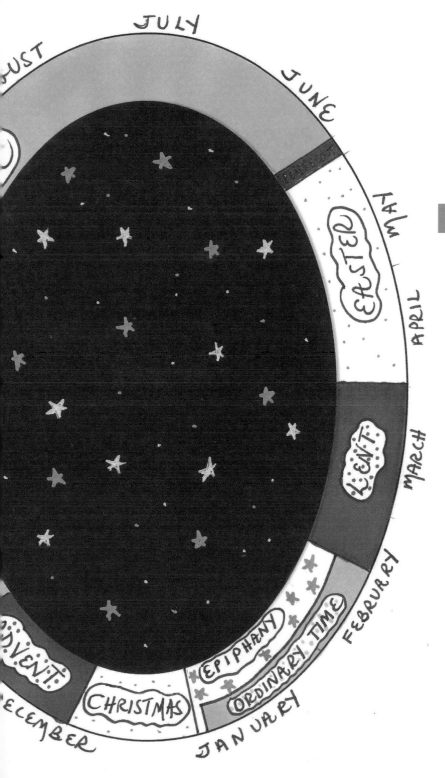

My prayer life expands and contracts. Bad things happen; good things happen. I grow older. Every year people, places, circumstances, and ideas inform what I bring to each liturgical season. The journey through the church year not only reunites me with my biblical and spiritual ancestors, but also places me in their lineage and on the path with millions of other "living stones" (1 Peter 2:5) who have walked with God.

I have never had a God-free life, but the liturgical calendar with its yearly rituals offers me a pilgrimage vocabulary and an entryway into spiritual practice. But be forewarned; in spite of its order and repetition, this pilgrimage is neither tame nor predictable. For me, it is often expansive and explosive: expansive because my understanding of the gospel grows; explosive because my life is often blown apart and rearranged by this "good news." The elliptical journey I take every day of every

year with God is more an extreme safari board game than a sweet and safe vacation.

St. Augustine (fourth–fifth century), St. Bernard of Clairvaux (eleventh–twelfth century), and twentieth-century British poet W. H. Auden all use the expression "the land of unlikeness" in their writing. For St. Augustine and St. Bernard the "land of unlikeness" seems to mean anything unlike God and therefore not desirable. In Auden's poem *For the Time Being: A Christmas Oratorio*, I hear something different. From Auden I understand "the land of unlikeness" as a place beyond human perception, unlike anything we have ever experienced before. The "land of unlikeness," for me, is the mystery and the wonder we encounter when we embark on a journey with God. In that land, as Auden says, we encounter "rare beasts" and have unimaginable adventures. It will be a wild pilgrimage.[1]

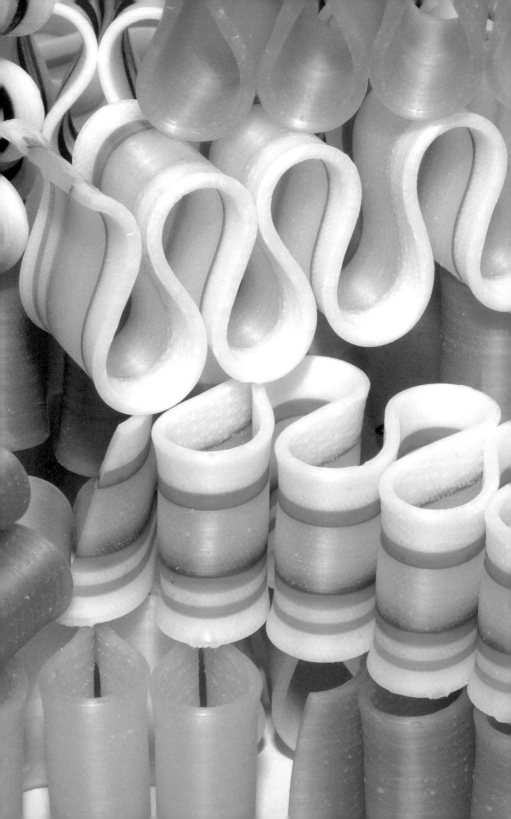

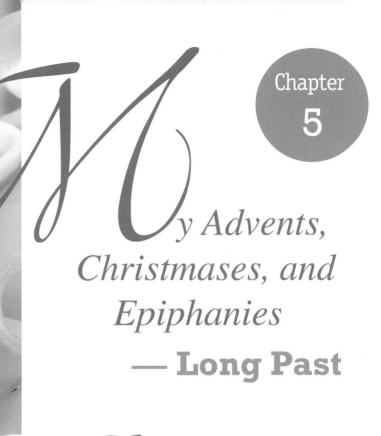

My Advents, Christmases, and Epiphanies
— **Long Past**

Advent

When I was a kid, Christmas trees started popping up in the neighbors' windows a week or two before December 25. Unlike now, when trees go up on Thanksgiving weekend, almost no one put a tree up before mid-December. My first memories of Christmas are of a live tree, tinsel, ribbon candy, and a spinning paper Christmas tree perched on a spike with pictures of ornaments on it.

I had never heard the word *Advent* before I met the Episcopalian, but I did love the week before Christmas. Waiting for Christmas has always been the best part for me. Once the tree was decorated with its fingerling-potato-sized colored lights, and the tinsel wars had ended (throw the tinsel from the steps or carefully place each strand?), the tree was mine.

In the split-level house where we lived, the tree stood in front of the picture window on the entry-level floor, the level with only one room—the formal living room. With its white wool rug, my mother's pride and joy, the room was designated for special communal occasions. It was the place where we played Candy Land® and Scrabble® and where my parents entertained friends for evenings of poker or bridge. It was also the room where the Fuller Brush man or the insurance man came to sell my mother quality home aids or death-defying policies. The living room was the place where I burrowed next to the couch and played paper dolls, spent hours thumbing through the *Britannica Junior Encyclopædia* and read my red leather-bound hardback King James Bible. It was my sanctuary.

When the Christmas tree had been put up and was lighted, it became my sanctuary within the sanctuary. I spent hours curled up under its branches. Sometimes I just lounged in the magic of the decorations and the silence. Sometimes, holiday music played on the hunky hi-fi. Every year my father brought home a new Firestone record album with titles like *Your Christmas Favorites.* The carols from the album filled me with joy and became part of my lifelong prayer and worship vocabulary.

In retrospect, the hours spent under the Christmas tree were my first Advents. Something unknown and bigger than me was about to happen. I was holding my breath and lying in wait, but there was no hurry. If I could have stopped time and captured those minutes in a jar I would have. When the tree went up and I was sprawled under it on the soft white rug, I was on holy ground.

Christmas

For many middle-class American children like me, Christmas was magical. My mother and I, wearing our better-than-Sunday-best, made the yearly trek to sit on Santa Claus's knee in the large downtown department store of our town. I don't remember making a list; I just remember the both awesome and scary experience of being in the presence of greatness dressed in red wool and white fur. A few weeks later on Christmas Day, unimagined gifts arrived for me under the tree: a baby doll with beautiful clothes, doll bunk beds, a Slinky®, Mr. Potato Head®, crayons, board games. . . .

This magical view of Christmas lasted until just about the time I reached double-digit age. My friends and I made lists of what we wanted for Christmas and gave them to our parents instead of to Santa Claus. Sometimes we received what we asked for, sometimes not. We expected our requests would be met. The "not" times were a disappointment, maybe even tinged with resentment. One friend and I learned how to prepare ourselves for the December 25 day of reckoning. I poked my head under beds and in closets looking for packages. She went through her parents' credit card receipts and carefully unwrapped and rewrapped presents. If we weren't going to get what we asked for, it was better to know ahead of time. Clearly, the magic was gone.

The year I turned sixteen was probably the final cut in the umbilical cord to a Santa Claus notion of Christmas. My parents had asked me what I wanted for Christmas. My only three requests were a hairdryer with a hood, a pair of fully lined aqua wool pants, and a multicolored pastel V-neck mohair sweater to complement the pants. The "asked for" items were expensive. I received all of them and nothing else.

After opening the long-longed-for and expected presents, I spent the rest of the morning facedown on my bed crying. There had been no surprises. My parents were to blame. I got nothing for Christmas, just three things. I wanted my mother to come into the room and feel sorry for me. She did come, but she was not sorry for me. She

claimed I was ungrateful. I was, but knew it only years later. When you get what you ask for, it's not always so great. There is no room for the unexpected magnanimity and creativity of others. There is no room for heartfelt and surprised gratitude. When you get what you ask for, it's not always what you really want. What I think I really hoped for was continuity from my Advent moments under the tree to what happened on Christmas Day and beyond. I got what I expected, and that was not enough.

Epiphany

I first heard of Epiphany as a season in the church year when I started to follow the liturgical calendar but gave it little attention or thought. As far as I knew it was a one-day blip on the church calendar, of little account in the scheme of things. On the Sunday nearest to January 6, the date of Epiphany, three people dressed in brocade bathrobes sometimes marched down the church aisle as we sang "We Three Kings." It seemed to signal the end of the Christmas holidays and nothing more. Epiphany was the day when the Advent wreath, the Christmas decorations, and the white Christmas hangings and vestments made their last hurrah.

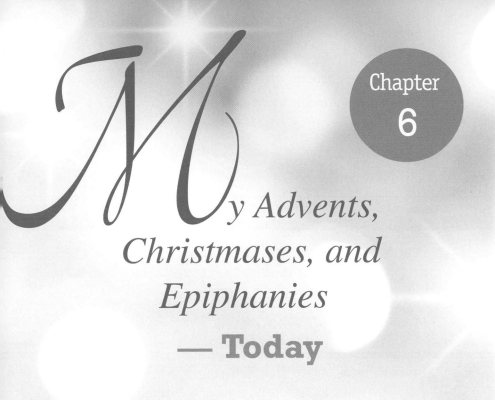

My Advents, Christmases, and Epiphanies — Today

A dvent, Christmas, and Epiphany are the opening acts and the pep rally for the rest of the liturgical year. They remind me to wake up, to watch, and to prepare for the events ahead. When late November rolls around, the liturgical year is just finishing its last days of summer and autumn's Ordinary Time.

The first Sunday in Advent, the Sunday closest to November 30, marks the Christian New Year. This is the time when I make my New Year's resolutions. Since most of my resolutions seem to be of a spiritual nature—"pray more, pay attention, be kind, love God, follow Jesus, close my mouth, open my heart . . ."—Advent seems more appropriate than January 1 for a fresh start, a new beginning.

During Ordinary Time, without any major Christian holidays and with vacations and the early months of the school year to distract me, the spiritual journey seems just so ordinary; I sometimes lose my way. Advent is the time for me to rejoin my pilgrim companions, to start again on the path through the calendar of Christian seasons and the wild walk with God.

Advent, Christmas, and Epiphany are seasons to dive into the story of Jesus. I do not need to make theological claims or sign off on doctrine to participate in its practices. "But what if I am unclear about the details of my theology?" I think the details of belief are less important than jumping in and marinating in the main premise: In both a worldly and miraculous way God broke into history in a special, radical event two-thousand-plus years ago in the unlikely form of a human infant.

The practices and rituals of Advent, Christmas, and Epiphany prepare me to receive the unanticipated gifts and surprises of Jesus's coming into the world. I enter the starting gate of the pilgrim's yearly journey at Advent and let the stories, images, feelings, and celebrations of the three seasons consume me. Conclusions, doctrine, and opinions can come later. For now, I want to marinate in the story and let it transform me. That much I know for sure.

The teachings and truth of history, science, and rational thought are important to my orderly, left-brained mind. But most of my favorite things in life are irrational: loving another human being, having children, eating chocolate, dancing, writing a book to convince people why Advent, Christmas, and Epiphany are the best party in town, and putting all of my stock in a Savior who appears weak and sees no reason to protect his ego or his person. If there is a season to suspend disbelief in the things I cannot see or prove, this is it. The entrance of God in human form into human life and history as a flesh-and-blood child is beyond rational thought, but it may be no less true than calculus and quarks.

The Nativity season opens my heart to the possibility of something new and wonderful and maybe even irrational. Madeleine L'Engle's poem "After Annunciation" captures this radical openness and wonder of this time of year.

This is the irrational season
When loves blooms bright and wild.
Had Mary been filled with reason
There'd have been no room for the child.[2]

Frameworks for the Nativity Season

A s my visual, oval calendars indicate, I rely on frameworks to help me organize my thoughts. In all parts of my life, frameworks provide parameters but offer freedom at the same time: years of ballet and modern dance classes taught me a vocabulary of movement. The vocabulary gave me the courage to join an improvisational dance group and to try my own choreography. Choreography emerges from the vocabulary as well as from the strictures of the dance space. Choreographing a liturgical dance for specific physical dimensions does not frustrate me. On the contrary, the particularities and peculiarities of the space provide a framework and guidelines within which to create. An altar rail, a set of wide stone stairs, and wooden choir stalls on either side of the available dance space are not so much limitations as they are props and partners in the dance.

As a doodler, I like the artistic challenge of choosing a four-inch by four-inch piece of paper and grabbing a black pen and three random colors from my basket of markers. Questions arise: What shapes work in this small space? Do these three colors work together, or do they need to be separated by white space or black lines? The limited space and limited color choices offer *unlimited* ways to play and draw on a sixteen-square-inch surface.

In my job as a community college math professor, frameworks and structures kept me organized and sane. In my fourteen years of teaching math at a community college, I never walked into the classroom without a written plan. Once inside the classroom, the plan did not necessarily legislate the work for the days. It freed me to pay attention to the needs of the students on a particular day and to improvise a new course of action.

I do not think I am alone in the need for structure. I taught pre-ballet and creative movement for several years to six- to eight-year-olds. If I turned on music and said, "Dance; do whatever you want," they were paralyzed. But if the instructions were more specific, the results were different. With a piece of chalk I drew a line. "Pretend there is a teeny-tiny tightrope from the piano to the corner of the room between the barres (those ballet handrails). There is a rushing river underneath. You need to get across the river on the rope. Move any way you want, but don't fall off!" Arms flailed and fluttered. Feet marched one before the other; heel to toe, toe to heel. Legs flew to left and right, helping tottering bodies to balance. Some children jumped or skipped or tiptoed backward. Some carefully bent their knees to crouch on the imaginary rope. The tight border of a single chalk line set the children free to dance.

In the same sort of way, I play with frameworks and structures to observe the seasons of Advent, Christmas, and Epiphany at home. Incorporating other people's rituals and creating practices of my own, the ideas in this book attempt to offer head-to-toe ways of experiencing the three seasons. These rituals and practices provide ways to learn, to worship, to pray, to celebrate, to be quiet, and to play. They provide some structures for a present-day immersion experience into the Nativity season, into the times and events surrounding Jesus's birth.

The following chapters are an invitation to you to create a Holy Advent, Christmas, and Epiphany of your own making. I hope they provide you with some structure and some tools for your own Advent, Christmas, and Epiphany journey. I hope they give you a jumping-off place for hosting and attending the best Nativity season party of your life.

*A*dvent

The Season
of Hope

> In the wilderness prepare the way of
> the Lord, make straight in the desert
> a highway for our God.
>
> —Isaiah 40:3

"Prepare, watch, wait, and keep awake" are a few of the many admonitions of Advent. Advent means "coming." As we prepare for Christmas, we remember Jesus's first coming into the world over two thousand years ago. Jesus was born into a time of political and social darkness. His people were in servitude to the Romans, not the first of their captors. They were waiting and watching and hoping for freedom from oppression. Jesus the Christ, the Messiah came.

So it's a done deal, right? The captives are free; the victory is won! Really? It doesn't always feel like freedom or victory. Jesus came; but there is still political and social darkness. People are still oppressed, hungry, and violated. Violence, greed, and hatred thrive. The Savior did not make it all right, at least not as the world imagined. "Things left undone" was not what was expected from the long-awaited Messiah.

Theologian Walter Brueggemann says Advent begins with a "*community of hurt.*"[3]

This community of hurt trusts in the One True God and becomes a "*community of hope.*"[4] Advent is full of paradoxes. In the midst of hurt there is hope. In the midst of fear there is faith. In the midst of darkness there is light. "Already" but "not yet" is a paradox of Christ's coming "already," but the transformation is "not yet" complete. St. John of the Cross used the expression "luminous darkness." The darkness around us is full of promise and light, but it takes Advent eyes and glasses to see it.

The world is still in Advent mode. Christians wait and long for a time when all will be well for everyone. The season of Advent is also about the second coming of Christ when all will *REALLY* be made right at the end of time. The two-dozen-plus days of Advent remind us that we are *still* waiting. But what the season of Advent tries to teach us is *how* to wait and to not lose heart, to live in hopeful patience. We rehearse during Advent the way to *wait* during the rest of the year, which is really the way to *live* during the rest of the year!

It is so easy for me to lose heart. Evidence of a restored kingdom seems scarce. After two thousand years of waiting, is anything really different? Christians who join me in this sort of discouragement often seem to draw two conclusions: (1) If anything in the world is going to change, humans have to do it. *Or* (2) nothing can be done about the sorry state of the world, but God will whisk us off to heaven when we die. But I think God calls us to a much more exciting challenge and promise.

We await and anticipate the transformation, but neither as relentless do-gooders nor as passive, restless heaven-bounders. We do not work in isolation under our own steam alone or twiddle our thumbs until the end times. The challenge is to trust in God's involvement with us now. "Something is about to happen,"[5] says theologian and preacher Thomas G. Long in his book of the same title. This is the Advent hope and cheer, the mantra of the crowd at the Nativity-season pep rally. *Something is about to happen* and God sends us instant-by-instant invitations to be in partnership with this world-transforming, kingdom-building happening.

The task for me is to recite and believe again and again the acclamation "God is up to something; something is about to happen"; "[God] has made known to us the mystery of his will, according to his good pleasure that he set forth in Christ, as a plan for the fullness of time, to gather up all things in him, things in heaven and things on earth" (Ephesians 1:9–10). What a "new world order" might look like will probably not meet my *expectations*. My *hope* is for something even greater than my expectations.

When we hope for God to finish the work begun in Jesus, we are not just wishing our lives away until the better days come. We are on a day-by-day pilgrimage in partnership with God. Joy mixes with sorrow. Faith and fear hold hands. Light shines in the darkness. *Something is about to happen*, and we don't know the time or date.

"This hidden plan will become apparent when time has run its course, when we can finally see that 'there

is only Christ, he is everything and he is in everything' (Colossians 3:11),"[6] says Franciscan priest Fr. Richard Rohr. As Advent people we are actively waiting for the revelation of this plan. We actively wait by joining the journey with Jesus as he says, "Follow me." "Jesus is the concrete personification in time of what has always been true, which is the *Christ* Mystery, or the 'anointing' of matter with eternal purpose,"[7] as Father Richard explains it.

*A*dvent
Practices
& Activities

My first intentional daily Advent practice was neither study nor prayer. It was an accidental art project.

I am not an artist; I cannot draw a cat or a dog (a refrain I have repeated for over a decade), but I love all of the paraphernalia and tools of my artist friends. Meandering through the aisles of my local art store and gawking at papers, paints, brushes, and unknown gadgets of the trade gives me head-to-toe tingles. I am a mere doodler and I own a bucketload of colored markers to indulge my playful habit.

In the mid-1980s, a friend named Cindy sent me an Advent mural calendar.[8] It looked like a sophisticated coloring

AN ADVENT ICON MURAL

WRITTEN BY
JEAN E. HAILER & C.E. VISMINAS

BY
SUMMERS & C.E. VISMINAS

book and included twenty-four pictures/icons of the prophets who foretold the coming of Jesus and of the important people in Jesus's life. The last four images were a three-part Nativity scene and included a place for a picture of me. Every day I read the explanatory paragraph, colored in one of the pictures with my markers, pasted it in the designated location on a large piece of paper, and watched the mural grow.

This daily practice was my first inkling of coloring and drawing as spiritual exercise and prayer. When I sat down to color I was quiet, calm, and fully focused on the picture—attentive! My hands, eyes, brain, and heart all participated in the experience. The half-hour coloring exercise helped me learn the cast of characters and enter into the story at the same time. At the end of Advent, not only was the finished calendar beautiful, but also it was a pictorial history of the birth of the Savior. And it was a record of my two dozen days of daily discipline.

I kept the two- by three-foot calendar and hung it on a door or wall every year in Advent. After many moves from city to city, it

went missing. At some point I bought another copy. I have stashed it away to use for some future Advent.

The year after I worked on the icon calendar, I purchased a Jesse tree calendar[9] from the same writers and illustrators. The Jesse tree shows the lineage of Jesus. It tells the story of Jesus's connection to the prophets and kings of Israel. Jesus is one of them. Fulfilling the words from Isaiah 11:1, "A shoot shall come out from the stump of Jesse, and a branch shall grow out of his roots," the Jesse tree is an abbreviated family tree from Creation to Jesus via Samuel, Jesse, David, Solomon, Hezekiah, and Joseph. Jesus as the adopted son of Joseph as well as the son of Mary, therefore, springs from the "root of Jesse."

My love of Advent was set in motion by my infatuation with these calendars twenty-five years ago.

The practices and activities described below are for you who are experimenting for the first time with Advent or are expanding your own love affair with this preparation time for Christmas. They are a combination of the serious and the playful. They cater to busy, word-weary, unfocused, and easily distracted persons. Some of them are daily practices; others are one-shot activities. Read through them and choose a few for yourself and your family. Don't try to tackle them all.

Some of the activities are educational and devotional. If those seem too heavy or serious, don't do them. Look for something less demanding and time-consuming. Some of the activities might seem superficial. Consider trying them anyway. You just might find that sprinkling purple sugar on your cereal every morning starts you off on another twenty-four hours in Advent mode. I have tried most of the activities here. I've done them with and without my children. I am a fool for Advent; I don't need to use my kids as an excuse.

Most of the activities are suitable for both adults and children. When children see the adults in their lives participate in Advent activities, they will understand the importance of the season. Advent is not just a way to keep the kids entertained until Christmas.

Advent is a season of reflection, prayer, meditation, and Scripture study, but it is also a time of intentional sensory experience. Jesus did not float in on a cloud. He came scrabbling through the birth canal of a human mother, gasping for breath in the midst of blood and bodily fluids. . . . Birth is not clean and tidy, it is earthy and sensory and sensual. I hope these activities and those in the Christmas and Epiphany sections will engage the head, the voice, the eyes, the hands, the feet, the heart, and the spirit. I hope they are inspirational but also a bit messy and earthy as well.

flaunt the color purple

Purple is the color most often associated with Advent. Some churches have switched to blue in recent years as a symbol of hope, expectation, and the Virgin Mary. But I like purple because it feels unusual, more regal. It symbolizes royalty, repentance, and reflection. Even though the blue hue of Advent is often vivid, I associate blue with ordinary things like uniforms and jeans. Go for blue if you want, but I'm sticking with purple, an extraordinary color.

Using purple throughout your house is not about creating another chance for decorative opportunities but is a visual reminder of the Advent season. Purple, for me, acts as a stoplight. It says: "Wait. It's not Christmas yet; slow down; pay attention to this time."

read the Scriptures & tell the stories

 Advent as a Christian season has been around for over a thousand years. Without the Scriptures and the stories there would be no season. Here is a short list of some of the **important readings** associated with Advent.

* **Isaiah 40:1–11, 42:1–9, 61:1–3, 63:16– 64:9a**—The hope and vision of God's restored kingdom for an oppressed people, the prophecy of a servant who will transform the nation under the One God

✳ **Matthew 1**—The genealogy of Jesus, Mary's pregnancy, an angel's appearance to Joseph in a dream

✳ **Luke 1**—The appearance of the angel Gabriel to Zechariah and Mary, the birth of John the Baptizer

✳ **John 1:6–9, 19–28**—The birth, ministry, and prophecies of John the Baptizer

✳ **Mark 13:31–37**—The warning to keep awake and alert for the end of heaven and earth

✳ **Luke 12:35–40**—The admonition to be watchful and ready for the coming of the Son of Man

✳ **1 Thessalonians 5:1–8**—The warning to keep awake for the day of the Lord

✳ **2 Peter 3:8–14**—The counsel to live holy lives in preparation for the fulfillment of God's kingdom promises

Read or tell the stories to the children in your house. Ask children to name or draw the objects or nouns they hear in the story. (Note: Here and in future activities I use the word *house* loosely. People live in all different kinds of physical spaces—apartments, dorms, trailers, mansions, mobile homes, cabins, tents, penthouses. . . . But it was easier to choose one word, so *house* it is. I tried *home* but it felt a little too fussy and decoratorish to me.)

In Advent **stories** or Christmas stories, ask questions (not just to the children—but to yourself and others) like: What do you hear? What do you smell? What do you feel? What do you taste? Who are the people in the story? What is your favorite part of the story? What is your least favorite part?

make or use advent calendars

My favorite activity during this season is using and/or creating an Advent calendar. The purpose of the Advent calendar is to count off the days until Christmas, to heighten our awareness of the passage of time.

The variety of **Advent calendars** is endless, and they are available online, in bookstores, and even in some grocery stores. The "old-fashioned," meaning twentieth-century and earlier versions, are made of paper and often include pictures of Santa Claus, the manger, or winter weather. Most calendars have twenty-four little paper doors; behind each is a picture or a Bible passage. Some doors open onto a piece of candy. (The "Bah! Humbug!" in me says, "No! Don't sweeten up Advent. Wait for Christmas.") Traditionally, every day, one family member opens the door for the day. By December 24, all of the doors but one are open. Christmas Day often has a fancier and larger door.

Advent calendars in recent years have morphed into **3-D works of art.** Made of felt, cardboard, wood, plastic, yarn, or just about any material, they hold small daily gifts or love notes. They can be recycled and used year after year.

Some websites offer **online Advent calendars.** Click on a date to reveal a picture, a passage of Scripture, or words of wisdom.

A favorite calendar used by my family was a large piece of red burlap attached on the top and bottom to two dowels. A piece of brown yarn with twenty-four loops gave us a zigzag pathway to follow as it made its way from the bottom of the calendar to the top, where it arrived at a simple felt stable with a star overhead. Each person in our family had a different-colored felt person attached to a Christmas-tree-ornament hanger. Every day we moved our person to the next loop until we arrived at the manger on Christmas Day. I loved the **journey theme** of the calendar.

Advent 2011

Sunday	Monday	Tuesday	Wednesday	Thursday	Friday	Saturday
NOV 27	28	29	30	DEC 1	2	3
4	5	6	7	8	9	10
11	12	13	14	15	16	17
18	19	20	21	22	23	24

My most recent Advent calendars have incorporated

Praying in Color ideas:

✳ **Create your own calendar template.** Draw or use a computer's table function to make a rectangular calendar template. A wall or desk calendar also works. One year I used purple construction paper with four-inch white stickers on it. Or draw a large seasonal symbol such as a tree, wreath, stained glass window, or star on paper.

✳ **Partition the calendar** into spaces equal to the number of days in Advent. Date the spaces. (Or date them each day as you go.) Unlike with the store-bought versions, you can determine the number of days on your calendar. I sometimes add a special spot for Christmas.

✳ **If you want larger spaces** in which to pray and draw, take your 8½-by-11 template to a copy store and blow it up on an 11-by-17 piece of card stock.

Here are some ways to
use your calendar:

❋ **Each day pray for a person.** Write the name of the person in the designated space for the day. Draw or doodle around the name, keeping the intention of your prayer in mind. If words come to you, pray them. If not, continue to draw. Add color with markers or colored pencils. Think of each stroke as a wordless prayer, as a time you spend with God and the person.

❋ **Write a word associated with Advent** in the space. Draw or doodle around the word as you look at it; ponder it; open your ears and your heart to it. Let God speak to you about and through the word.

❋ **Just draw each day without an agenda.** Use this as a quiet, listening, and waiting time. Instead of saying, "I'll pray today for ten minutes," I jokingly say, "I'll pray for an inch by an inch and a half."

❋ **Provide young children with art supplies** they can use to fill in their calendars: small pieces of colored paper to paste, glitter, large markers, crayons, and stickers. You can also give children a large, new page each day with a different shape: star, wreath, snowman, camel, or other seasonal shape. Save each day's drawing, and at the end of the season, put them together as the child's personal Advent calendar booklet.

❋ **Four-inch, round stickers work well** for a daily drawing space for children (and adults). The finished stickers can be placed on a big piece of poster board or decorative paper each day.

String a mini clothesline along a wall or across a space where no one will run into it. Hang small envelopes on the line with tiny clothespins. The envelopes and clothespins are available for purchase online. Each day, draw on one envelope. Write a word or a picture. Take turns. **Ask each family member to put their loose change—pennies, dimes, nickels, quarters, or even some dollar bills)—into the envelope of the day.** At the end of Advent collect and count the money. Send it to the food bank, animal shelter, or another charity.[12]

Create advent wreaths

An Advent wreath marks the weeks before Christmas with four candles—three purple (or blue) and one pink. Four purple candles is also a common choice. On each of the four Sundays of Advent, light a new candle; every day during that week light the same candle. On the second Sunday of Advent, light a new purple candle as well as the one from week one. Light the pink candle on the third Sunday of Advent. The pink candle represents the halfway point to Christmas and offers a glimpse of the light soon to come. On the fourth Sunday of Advent, light all of the candles.

Say a prayer with the lighting of each candle. Traditional prayers can be found in books and online.

variations

Find a time when the people in your house can gather together, if only for a minute, to **light the candles.** With sports, extracurricular activities, and nontraditional family configurations, a nightly dinner, a common time to light the Advent wreath, might not be the norm in your household. For families with small children or even couples, bedtime might be the logical gathering time.

✳ **Place the wreath where people will walk by it** with some frequency. This can be in a living area, the kitchen, or someplace as mundane as a hallway outside of the bathroom. Even when it is not lit, the wreath will be a reminder of the season.

✳ **Create a basket of one-line prayers** or verses of Scripture on folded pieces of paper. At each lighting of the candles, pull a prayer from the basket. For families with children, one child chooses a prayer and reads it (alone or with help from a parent). After the prayer is read, post the prayer on a wall or bulletin board. Or hang it on the tree or on a mock clothesline.

Here are a few examples of one- or two-line verses and prayers from both the Hebrew and Christian Scriptures. For a longer list, see the appendix. These verses reflect the paradoxical and conflicting emotions of Advent: hope, despair, longing, praise, sorrow, excitement, trust, fear. . . . They speak of our hunger for freedom and refuge. They witness to God's faithfulness and promises.

✳ **Psalm 80:2a–3** *Stir up your might, and come to save us! Restore us, O God; let your face shine, that we may be saved.*

✳ **Isaiah 60:2** *For darkness shall cover the earth, and thick darkness the peoples; but the Lord will arise upon you, and his glory will appear over you.*

✳ **Jeremiah 8:18–19** *My joy is gone, grief is upon me, my heart is sick. Hark, the cry of my poor people from far and wide in the land: "Is the Lord not in Zion? Is her King not in her?"*

✳ **Malachi 3:1** *See, I am sending my messenger to prepare the way before me, and the Lord whom you seek will suddenly come to his temple. The messenger of the covenant in whom you delight—indeed, he is coming, says the Lord of hosts.*

✳ **Matthew 3:3** *This is the one of whom the prophet Isaiah spoke when he said,*

"The voice of one crying out in the wilderness: 'Prepare the way of the Lord, make his paths straight.'"

✳ **Mark 13:32–33** *But about that day or hour no one knows, neither the angels in heaven, nor the Son, but only the Father. Beware, keep alert; for you do not know when the time will come.*

✳ **Luke 2:11** *This will be a sign for you: you will find* a child wrapped in bands of cloth and lying in a manger.

✳ **John 1:1–2** *In the beginning was the Word, and the Word was with God, and the Word was God. He was in the beginning with God.*

✳ **Romans 13:12** *The night is far gone, the day is near. Let us then lay aside the works of darkness and put on the armor of light.*

To make the Advent wreath you can purchase an "Advent wreath starter kit." Different styles include a circular metal frame or a round Styrofoam form with four designated places for the candles. Weave greens and ribbons in and out of the form. For me this is an artistic and aesthetic challenge, so I have adapted the wreath to match my skill level.

variations

 Use four **candlestick holders** instead of a preformed wreath. Use matching or mismatched holders. Dollar stores carry them for $1. Place them in a circle, a line, or any helter-skelter configuration. Add real greens from your yard or inexpensive artificial ones. Purple paper chains or ribbon can substitute for greenery.

Use four votive candles,

four mismatched candles, or the stubs of candles
recycled from previous years.

**If candles and wreaths are not available,** make candles from construction paper. Draw lines on each candle equal to the number of days in Advent. Each day, snip off the bottom of the candle.

set up Advent/ Christmas trees

I enjoy the challenge and delayed gratification of waiting until at least December 20 to put up our Christmas tree. The waiting is not easy, because I love my Christmas tree. The year my husband and I were married, a friend gave us ten ornaments for our first holiday season as a couple. The ornaments were all animals and people. This became the theme of all of our subsequent trees. Every year when I unpack the hippos, angels, unicorns, fishermen, dancers, and all manner of creature, I welcome my longtime friends back for their yearly appearance.

If you want to delay the onset of Christmas decorations but meet some family resistance, go ahead and buy or assemble your tree at your usual time. Put the tree in its stand, water it (if it's real), and tease your family into trying one of several things.

variations

 Leave the tree bare. The sight of an undecorated tree reminds us that we are still waiting and hoping for the arrival of Christmas with its celebration, glitz, and glamour.

 String the tree with **purple lights.** Or put lights on a large houseplant.

 Cover it with **white lights.**

 String the lights you will use for Christmas. Add an ornament a day. If you have an abundance of ornaments, let each child or person in the family **hang one or two ornaments each day.**

 Create a **Chrismon tree.** Chrismon was the name Frances Kipps Spencer at Ascension Lutheran Church in Danville, Virginia, gave to the symbolic ornaments she designed for a tree in the sanctuary of the church in 1957. Typical symbols on a Chrismon tree are crosses, stars, doves, candles, shells, keys, and any kind of Christian symbol. The ornaments are white and gold. I have seen paper, embroidered, needlepoint, and Styrofoam ornaments. Use your imagination. The ornaments can be the

elegant creations of serious artists or the handiwork of small children. Online and book resources are available with directions and patterns.

 Create a **"Hope" tree.** Have a basket of shipping/price tags or small pieces of paper with clothespins near the tree. Invite visitors, friends, and family members to write their Hopes on the paper and tie them to the tree.

Have each family member make a **paper chain** throughout Advent, adding one link a day until December 24. Use whatever colors of paper you like. Hang the chains on the tree and watch them lengthen day by day. Leave them on the tree for Christmas as a reminder of the long, symbolic wait during Advent and the long wait of our spiritual ancestors for a savior.

 A Norfolk Island pine, often sold at grocery stories and only about two to three feet high, works well for **small spaces** or when travel means putting up a big tree is a hassle.

 If you can't wait until Christmas Eve to decorate your Christmas tree with Christmas ornaments, try to **delay** its appearance until at least mid-December. If you are accustomed to a Thanksgiving weekend of decorating, the delay of two weeks might be a family Advent exercise in waiting.

watch plants grow

One way to teach children (and adults) about *watching* and *waiting*—but not waiting in vain—is with bulbs.

From a garden or big-box home store, purchase an amaryllis or several paperwhite narcissus

bulbs.

* **Fill a container with potting soil** or stones. Plant the bulb in the soil or stones with about half of the bulb showing above the surface. Place the pot near a sunny window and water frequently. Amaryllis bulbs often come with their own pot and a special growing medium.

* **I like to plant narcissus** bulbs in a clear glass container. Watching the roots spread downward and outward as the plant shoots upward is a visual lesson in grounding and growing as a joint venture.

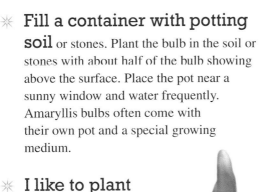

✳ **Start the bulbs** on the first day of Advent.
Gentle daily watering functions as a form of Advent
discipline. Somewhere in the latter days of Advent
or on one of the twelve days of Christmas, the plants
will start to flower.

✳ **In my catalog of olfactory memorabilia,**
the smell of paperwhites will always signal
Advent (or Christmas) for me.

There is irony in this process called *forcing* bulbs.
We wait for our children to grow up; we wait for
retirement; we wait for God to answer our prayers.
. . . None of these spiritual *waitings* can actually be
forced.

create a
progressive crèche

Nativity sets, or crèches, come in all shapes and sizes. They can include straw-filled cribs, baby Jesuses, Marys, Josephs, Wise Men or Magi, camels, shepherds, cows, sheep, and donkeys. People put them on tables or mantels at the same time they decorate the rest of their homes.

 Decide where you want to put the Nativity set.

Place the animals there. Add a little greenery or fake hay. If Jesus's bed is separate from Jesus, include it with the animals.

✳ **Place Mary and Joseph together** away from the scene—in a far corner of the room or in another room. Let them take the journey through Advent toward the manger with you. Move them a little closer each day. On Christmas Eve move them to the manger. Until Christmas Eve, hide the baby Jesus or find a way to attach him to Mary.

✳ **Hide the shepherds**, Magi, and camels far away from the Nativity scene—maybe even in storage. Let the shepherds arrive on Christmas Day, but keep the kings or Magi away until January 6! If you want the shepherds and kings in sight before Christmas, place them far from the scene and move them a little closer each day. Moving them closer each day is an appropriate task for a young child.

variations

Cut two-inch pieces of yellow or tan yarn. Whenever you or your children **notice an act of kindness during the day,** invite them to add a piece of "hay" to Jesus's bed.[13]

do unto others

In the midst of Christmas planning and preparation I often forget anyone outside the inner circle of my family and friends. Advent is a good time to share our abundance and to start a regular habit of giving to others.

As a family, **study the many wonderful local and national charities.** Let each person in the family choose a charity. Make a donation in their honor or in honor of a friend or relative. Organizations such as Heifer Project, St. Jude Children's Hospital, Save the Children, Toys for Tots, or Make-A-Wish might interest the people in your house.

Offer to help older relatives and neighbors set up their tree or hang Christmas lights. Offer shopping assistance to someone who cannot drive a car or does not know how to order gifts online.

Place a large basket near your crèche or tree. **Make a daily donation** into the basket from your kitchen shelves or the grocery store of canned and dry foods. Alternate days for family members' deposits or let each person choose and put in a daily item. At the end of Advent, pack the food in bags or boxes and deliver it together to the local food bank.

Explore the **Angel Tree ministry** of Prison Fellowship. Angel Tree organizes the distribution of presents for children whose parent or parents are in prison. Angel Tree provides churches, organizations, or families with the names and specific requests of a child. Families or individuals purchase the requested presents and deliver them to a location for distribution or at an Angel Tree party for the children. You or your children get to be active participants in fulfilling the specific Christmas wishes of others.

practice hopefulness

Advent emphasizes the anticipation that something exciting and life-changing is about to happen. Christians really believe "God is up to something"! Hopefulness is a practiced attitude. It takes diligence to not be overwhelmed by the violence, injustice, poverty, and sorrow in the world. Some people think God is up to something when they see bad things happen. But I believe God is in the business of salvation and encourages change for the good. What is the evidence you see that God is "up to something"?

Hang a white board or piece of **poster board** paper on a wall in a communal space.

❋ **Ask family members to write or draw** the signs of God's presence in the world and in their lives. What has God done in your life today? What good is happening in the world? Teach your eyes and ears to look for the good stuff, for the signs of creation and new life.

❋ **If you're not comfortable with just noticing the good,** use two pieces of poster board—one white, one gray. Write the signs of doom and gloom on one, the signs of hope and light on the other. Cut out or print both troubling and hopeful articles from the newspaper. Paste or pin them onto the poster board.

learn the vocabulary of Advent

A dvent readings and meditations are full of rich and sometimes paradoxical words. *Darkness and light, despair and hope, wait and hurry* are examples of the complex Advent concepts.

 Hang a large white board or piece of **poster board** paper on a wall in a communal space.

✳ **Write the words of Advent on separate pieces of paper** and put the slips of paper in a bag or basket. If you don't know many words, go online or read Isaiah 35 or 40. Use some of the words from the drawing at the beginning of the chapter.

✳ **Each day, ask someone to pick a piece of paper** from the collection of words and write it on the board. Write them anywhere on the paper or board, not necessarily in an orderly list. Use colored markers to make them stand out from each other.

✳ **Have a simple discussion about the word.**

✳ **Add a new word every day** to the growing collection. Viewing the words on a daily basis implants them into our long-term vocabulary.

✳ **If you want to delve deeper** into the words, free-write a page about the word. Or draw around it and let it speak to you.

variations

Another way to **teach the vocabulary** is to write the words on strips of paper instead of on a whiteboard or poster board. Hang the words on the tree. Or turn each piece of paper into a link of a paper chain with the words facing outward.

pray an Advent word

This is a prayer exercise for adults and teens.

Pick an intriguing, troubling, or interesting word from your Scripture reading or from the jumble of words on the Advent drawing at the beginning of the section.

※ **Write the word** in the middle of an unlined sheet of white paper. For about five minutes, write down everything you associate with the word, even if it is silly or far-fetched. Write words or phrases. Brainstorm. Include everything that comes to mind. Do not edit.

※ **Get a new sheet of plain paper.** Write the same word again in the middle of the page. This time don't think. Listen to what the word has to tell you about itself. Ask God what you need to know about the word. Then quiet your brain. While you are listening, draw or doodle on the page, around the word. Draw with a pen. Use colored pencil or markers and add color, if you like. Keep your hand moving while you listen. If you hear other words or even the same words you wrote before, write them down. Do this for five to ten minutes.

※ **Have a conversation with God.** Ask God about the word. This also might be a time for questions or adoration. It is not a time to pray for others. It's a time for you to be with God. Keep drawing on the same page while you pray. Write down your thoughts, questions, or prayers during the conversation. Another option is to put down the pen and colors and just sit still.

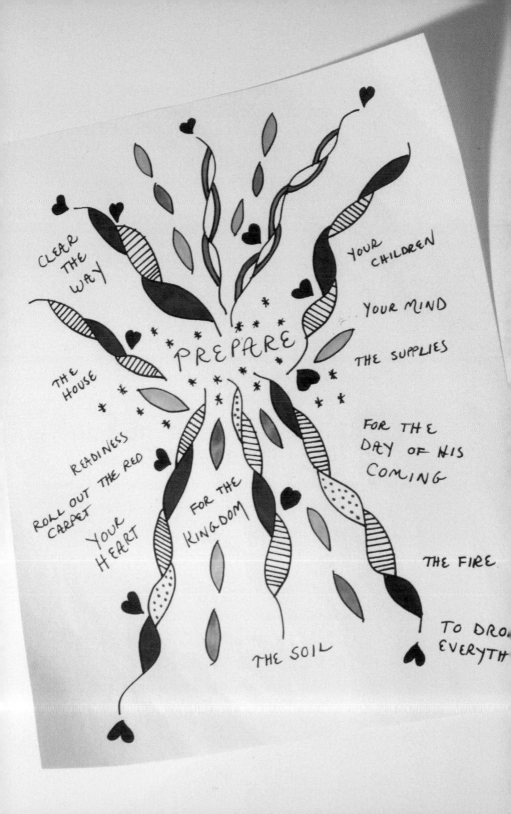

PREPARE

CLEAR THE WAY

THE HOUSE

READINESS

ROLL OUT THE RED CARPET

YOUR HEART

FOR THE KINGDOM

THE SOIL

YOUR CHILDREN

YOUR MIND

THE SUPPLIES

FOR THE DAY OF HIS COMING

THE FIRE

TO DRO… EVERYTH…

✳ **After several minutes of conversation** with God, just close your eyes, sit still, and breathe. For the next few minutes let whatever happens happen. Maybe you will just be quiet and relax into the silence. Maybe you will be antsy. Maybe you will have a great "aha." Let it be. Take a deep breath when you are finished and say "Amen."

(The above exercise is from my book *Praying in Color: Drawing a New Path to God—Portable Edition.* Others ideas in the book can be adapted for Advent.)

sing songs and chants

Choose one of the one-line verses in the Advent wreath section and sing it. Make up a tune and tweak it until you are happy with it. No music training necessary. Just sing. If you like the result, share it with others.

Of all of the Advent hymns, "O Come, O Come Emmanuel (or Immanuel)" is probably my favorite. You can **learn and sing a verse a week.**[14]

O Come, O Come, Immanuel

5 O come, O Key of David, come
and open wide our heavenly home.
Make safe for us the heavenward road
and bar the way to death's abode.

6 O come, O Bright and Morning Star,
and bring us comfort from afar!
Dispel the shadows of the night
and turn our darkness into light.

7 O come, O King of nations, bind
in one the hearts of all mankind.
Bid all our sad divisions cease
and be yourself our King of Peace.

Advent Chant

This is one of my favorite songs for Advent. It is simple enough for children to learn and works well as a round. Sing it every night during Advent at your wreath lighting or as a bedtime song with children.[15]

ADVENT CHANT

Phil Porter

Twi-light then dark-ness. Night falls and can-dles glow. Gent-ly sur round-ing us a— new birth of hope. Watch - ing, wait - ing, a - wak - en a new birth of hope.

This chant can be sung as a two-part round, divided at the numbered bars.

Listen to **part 1 of Handel's *Messiah*.** Part 1 sings the Advent and Christmas story. The libretto, or words, comes directly from the Hebrew and Christian Scriptures—from the prophecies of Isaiah, Haggai, Malachi, and Zechariah to the Gospels of Matthew and Luke.

Advent is a good time to **learn and teach the songs and carols of Christmas.** Since most schools do not teach Christian carols, home (or church) is where children will learn them.

Caroling in the neighborhood with your family and with a group of friends is a way to reinforce and share the music. Walking and singing plant the songs in the body one footstep at a time. Wonderful musical albums are available for listening and learning new and old carols. Some are geared specifically toward Advent.

learn the cast of characters

Gabriel, Zechariah, Mary, Elizabeth, and Joseph are important characters in the Advent narrative. Try some varied ways to learn their stories.

 Read the stories of Gabriel, Zechariah, Mary, Elizabeth, and Joseph in Matthew 1 and Luke 1–2.

 Talk about angels. What is an angel? What is the purpose of angels? What might one look like? Promote angels as powerful creatures rather than the sweet, chubby, and cherubic characters of Valentine's Day cards. Look for pictures of angels online. Which ones fit your image of biblical angels?

Give a character's name
to each reading-age person in your family. Ask them
to search online for the character and see what they
can learn. Report back to the others.

 After you have learned about the character, write
a **tweet** (140 characters or less including
spaces and punctuation) or a three-sentence story as
a summary. Write the tweets on a computer or use
large sticky notes and post them around the house.
The short, tight structure of these two forms helps to
recall the story in a concise and playful way. Here is
an example of a tweet for Zechariah:

> *Z struck speechless when he pooh-poohed the angel's prophecy
> of fatherhood. His first words after nine silent months:
> "His name is John."* (137 characters and spaces)

The writing does not have to be complicated or elegant.
Here is a three-sentence story about Mary:[16]

> *The angel Gabriel visited a teenaged girl named Mary.*
> *He told her she would have a baby by the Holy Spirit.*
> *Mary said, "Okay, I'll do it."*

 Say together and/or **learn by heart
the Song of Mary,** also called the
Magnificat. From Luke 1:46–55, these are Mary's

words to her cousin Elizabeth, the mother of John the Baptist. Alternate voices at the asterisks. The Magnificat is one of the passages I know by heart and keep in my spiritual toolbox for times when I cannot find words for my prayers.

My soul proclaims the greatness of the Lord,
*my spirit rejoices in God my Savior; ***
*   for he has looked with favor on his lowly servant.*
*From this day all generations will call me blessed: ***
*   the Almighty has done great things for me,*
*   and holy is his Name.*
*He has mercy on those who fear him ***
*   in every generation.*
*He has shown the strength of his arm, ***
*   he has scattered the proud in their conceit.*
*He has cast down the mighty from their thrones, ***
*   and has lifted up the lowly.*
*He has filled the hungry with good things, ***
*   and the rich he has sent away empty.*
*He has come to the help of his servant Israel, ***
*   for he has remembered his promise of mercy,*
*The promise he made to our fathers, ***
*   to Abraham and his children for ever.*[17]

Download artwork and

pictures of Gabriel, Zechariah, Mary, Elizabeth, and Joseph. Ask children to notice what they see in the paintings. Tape the pictures around the house. Don't forget to notice along with your children. The artwork you choose might be familiar to you, but there are always new details to notice.

Learn about these biblical characters with **your voice and body.** The following movement pieces tell the stories of some of the Advent heroes and heroines. The Zechariah and Mary pieces[18] are by my friend Roy DeLeon, author of *Praying With the Body: Bringing the Psalms to Life*, published by Paraclete Press. It can be danced as a group or as a solo meditation. Have one person read a line out loud and do the movement at the same time. The group responds by echoing the words and the gestures. The leader goes to the next line and the group copies again. These movement pieces can be repeated over and over again throughout Advent. If they are memorized and practiced enough, a group can do them together without a leader.

Zechariah

In the days of King Herod in Judea,	There was a priest named Zechariah.	Once when Zechariah was offering incense in the sanctuary,	An angel appeared.	Zechariah was terrified.

Hands on the side	Hands in prayer pose	Hands lifted up, offering incense	Flap arms up and down	Bend knees, hands on crown of head

"Do not be afraid," said the angel.

Arms softly extended, palms down to calm Zechariah

"Your prayer has been heard."

Your wife Elizabeth will bear a son and you will name him John."

"He will give you much joy and gladness."

"He will be great in God's eyes."

"Zechariah doubted this news."

Hands in prayer, then lift up showing answer from God

Hands on belly

Lift arms and one leg. Repeat on other leg

Step one foot forward and throw arms back to open heart

Hands on ears, shaking head

He pushed away the angel's message.

"I am old, and so is my wife. How can this be true?"

The angel replied: "I am Gabriel."

"I am sent by God to bring you this good news."

"Because you did not believe my words,"

Hands pushing from the heart

Slump down, hands on old knees

Hands akimbo, feet wide, angry

One hand shoots up pointing to heaven, then other hand pointing to Zechariah

Both hands pointing to Zechariah

"You will be mute, unable to speak until the day these things occur."

Both hands cover mouth

When Zechariah left the sanctuary, he motioned with his arms. But he could not speak.

One hand moving while other points to mouth/throat

Mary

The angel Gabriel was sent by God To the town of Nazareth in Galilee

To a young woman, a virgin, named Mary. Mary was engaged to a man whose name was Joseph.

Gabriel said to Mary, "Greetings, favored One."

"The Lord is with you."

Hands lifted above the head 45°

Hands in prayer

Hands lifted up, elbows bent

Arms extended, palms turned down in blessing

Mary was troubled and perplexed by these words.

But the angel said: "Do not be afraid, Mary."

"You have found favor with God."

"You will conceive a child and give birth to a son."

"His name will be called Jesus."

Bend knees, hands on crown of head

Arms extended, palms pushing away fear

One arm extended toward heaven, other extended toward Mary

Hands on belly

Arms extend to Mary, elbows bent

"He will be great and will be called the Son of the Most High."

Both arms extended to side at shoulder height, palms turned upward

"He will reign over the house of Jacob forever." · *"And his kingdom will have no end."* · *Mary said to the angel, "How can this be? I am still a virgin."* · *The angel said to her: "The Holy Spirit will come upon you."*

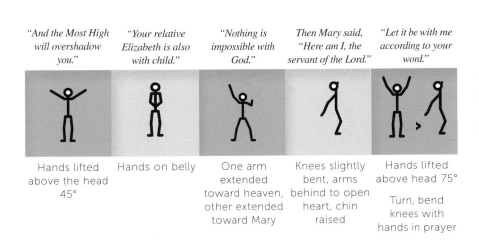

Arms make a roof over head · Arms extended sideways at about 45° · Bend knees, rest chin on hands · Leg lifted behind, arms extended backward

"And the Most High will overshadow you." · *"Your relative Elizabeth is also with child."* · *"Nothing is impossible with God."* · *Then Mary said, "Here am I, the servant of the Lord."* · *"Let it be with me according to your word."*

Hands lifted above the head 45° · Hands on belly · One arm extended toward heaven, other extended toward Mary · Knees slightly bent, arms behind to open heart, chin raised · Hands lifted above head 75°

Turn, bend knees with hands in prayer

✳ **Write text and create movement stories** for other characters.

make room for quiet time and prayer

Since Advent is a season of waiting and contemplation, give children and adults an old-fashioned egg timer filled with salt or sand. Invite them to have their own private time with the Advent wreath or the lighted "Christmas" tree. Challenge them to **three minutes of silence.** If it works, go for six minutes. The egg timer is a quiet alternative to a phone or kitchen timer. It also provides a visual of the falling grains for an exercise in watching. For additional time, turn the egg timer over for another three minutes of quiet and solitude.

Pray an **Advent breath prayer.**[19] Breath prayers are one-line prayers with a name for God and a request. The prayers are said over and over again until they become as natural as your breath. It is a way to move toward "praying unceasingly." Some people pray one line on the inhale, one line on the exhale. You can grab your breath prayer whenever you need to pray—especially when you can't think of what to say—and pray it as many times as you like. Here are some Advent-specific breath prayers:

Come, Lord Jesus, come.

Come quickly, longed-for Savior.

Beloved One, be patient with me.

Creator God, heal our world.

Father-Mother God, rescue me from despair.

God of light, break into my darkness.

Holy One, repair our world.

Create your own, using any source that inspires you and helps you speak to God. Help children to create simple, one-line prayers.

Spend some time alone with God. Here is a visual and kinesthetic way to set the stage for some quiet prayer time. Grab plain paper, a black pen, and colored markers or pencils. Write the word you like to use for God in the middle of or at the top of the page. Brainstorm all of the things on your mind and heart. Write down your hopes for the holiday and your hopes for the world and life in general. Write down the names of people you are worried about. Add things for which you are grateful and things for which you are sorry. Complete thoughts and complete sentences are not necessary. Nobody but you needs to know what you mean. You do not need to edit your thoughts, your organization, or your spelling.

When you have written all of your head and heart prayer concerns on the page and your mind feels empty, get a clean sheet of paper. Write your God name on the new page. Start to draw or doodle around the name. Focus on the name. Let your hand do what it wants. Imagine you and God are sitting together in a room in silence. (This is exactly what is happening.) Don't think; let your mind rest and just listen. If other prayer thoughts come to you, write them down. If not, enjoy the silence.

doubt clean air open mind fear house
downsizing
new work home good public education
ease play laziness
healing GOD sons
surround me singing family courage
depression peace in the world
community direction unbelief
sunsets friends sobriety for
church MBCD
children dancing
cooperation in government adventure judgmental
open heart

The list of **wonderful books and websites** about Advent grows each year. Choose theology, Scripture study, or daily reflections to enhance your prayer and meditation.

what about
Santa Claus?

I have **no expert answer** to this question. My husband and I never took our children to sit on Santa's lap, but neither did we deny his existence. Our sons heard stories and songs about Santa. There are pros and cons to promoting the notion of Santa Claus. Santa brings a sense of play, wonder, delight, and joy. And it's just plain fun to surprise children with gifts from an unknown source. But Santa can also encourage greed and self-centeredness. The focus moves from Jesus to presents in a flash.

In a lecture I heard years ago, a C. S. Lewis scholar gave some input I had not considered. He suggested that it was important for children to believe in Santa Claus because it sharpened and prepared their imaginations for the even more wonderful and irrational miracle of Jesus. Believing in Santa Claus was a rehearsal for believing in Jesus. This is an intriguing idea, but it can be confusing to children.

If the tradition for welcoming Santa Claus is a plate of cookies and a glass of milk (carrots for the reindeer), **ask children what would they do for Jesus** if they knew he was coming to their house in the middle of the night. Would they provide food, a blanket, or a map to the bathroom? How would they prepare a place for him near a fire or at the kitchen table?

 Read the story of **the real St. Nicholas,** a fourth-century bishop in Asia Minor who is said to have given bags of gold to three girls to keep them from prostitution and to have put coins in the shoes of needy children. He was the prototype for the contemporary Santa Claus. History or legend, the story is a seasonal example of generosity and giving. Nicholas's story is available for children and adults.[20]

more activities for busy houses

 At the beginning of Advent have a **family dinner** at which children and adults ask questions. "Why is Advent a season different

from other seasons?" "What does the word *Advent* mean?" "What do we do during Advent?" "Why isn't our Christmas tree up yet?" "Why do we have purple candles?" "Why isn't Jesus in the manger?" "How long do we have to wait before Christmas?" Jewish families ask similar questions at a Passover seder. Use the questions as a lead-in for discussion. They can be a way to explain to children the uniqueness of Advent and the importance of preparation time before Christmas. Let children and adults try to answer the questions. Answers can be short and open-ended.

Put **purple lights** on the outside of your house or in your yard. They might be a good conversation starter with your neighbors.

Advent is a season of both **darkness and light.** Sometimes we jump right to the light and avoid the darkness. Gather the members of your household and find the darkest place in the house—the basement, a big closet, a place with room-darkening shades. Try to remove all signs of light. Sit in the dark room together but apart. Be silent for a minute or two. Then ask the question: "What do you notice about sitting in the dark?" Then try sitting in the dark again, this time holding hands. Ask the "noticing" question again. Then light a candle; be silent, and ask the "noticing" question again.[21]

On a clear, dark night, go outside and **look at the stars.** If it's cold, bundle up the kids in pajamas and blankets and look up and out. What do you notice? Ask children what they see in the sky and around them. Paying attention and watching are two of the habits we cultivate during Advent.

 ## Create an Advent wall.

Temporarily remove pictures and pull out furniture to make a communal space where you can hang drawings, words, Advent calendars, writings, and downloaded copies or prints of famous Nativity paintings.

 Hang **a map of the world** in a high-traffic zone: the kitchen, bathroom, or living area. Mark Bethlehem with a star or circle. A map doesn't have to be fancy. Just download and print one from the Internet. A map is both an educational tool and a way to picture where others live around the world. Hang a separate map of the Holy Land on the wall, too. Find Nazareth and find Bethlehem. Imagine the routes by which Mary and Joseph made their way to Bethlehem from their hometown.

Create a stack of **Advent napkins.** Take white paper napkins and dot them with a larger purple marker. The purple dots are just another visual reminder of Advent. Very young children can do this while older siblings work on their Advent calendars. Paper towels are a substitute for napkins.

 Make or buy **purple granulated sugar.** Sprinkle it on cereal or ice cream for a special treat during Advent.

Purchase an Advent donkey, sheep, or **camel "piggy" bank.** Ask family members to put something in the bank each day. At the end of Advent collect and count the money. Take or send it to the food bank, animal shelter, or another charity.

Eat dinner by **candlelight.** Battery-operated votive candles are another option. The candles, real or not, create an Advent atmosphere, emphasizing the classic Advent theme of light in the darkness. An added bonus, the children *and* the adults in our family seem to behave better in low light.

Create a **family art table** or corner. Supply it with paper, colored markers, crayons, glitter, rulers, cookie cutters—use your imagination. Put sheets of paper or large Post-its on the wall. Let people come up with ideas for activities.

Along with snowflakes and Christmas symbols, **paint some Advent words** on your windows with removable craft paint. Let your neighbors know about Advent. Create an Advent banner and tape it on an outside wall or window.

Learn about the lives of the other saints whose feast days

fall during Advent. Whether fact or legend, their stories and witness have lessons to teach and are important to many Christians around the world.

✷ **Our Lady of Guadalupe** is called the Patroness of the Americas and Mexico. In 1531, Juan Diego, a Christian Aztec Indian saw a vision of Mary the mother of Jesus in Mexico. She healed Juan's uncle, appeared to him as an Aztec princess, and gave him roses to deliver to the bishop. When Juan opened his cloak, or tilma, to deliver the roses, the image of Mary was emblazoned on the tilma. Her feast day is December 12 in the United States.

✷ **St. Lucy** or St. Lucia is a popular saint throughout Europe, especially in Scandinavia. She lived in Syracuse in the fourth century and was put to death for being a Christian. Her name means "light." Little else is known for sure. Legend says torturers blinded her, but her eyes and sight were restored by God. Another legend claims she wore a wreath of evergreen on her head with candles to light the way as she brought food to persecuted Roman Christians. She is the patron saint of the blind. Her feast day is December 13.

*C*hristmas
The Season
of Love

For a child has been born for us, a son
given to us; authority rests upon his
shoulders; and he is named Wonderful
Counselor, Mighty God, Everlasting Father,
Prince of Peace.

—ISAIAH 9:6

Alleluia! Christ is born. The Savior is born indeed!" Let the party begin. Christmas is the culmination and fulfillment of our Advent waiting. Christmas celebrates the birth of Jesus, the promised Savior who has come to free the world, liberate the oppressed, and set the captives free. We celebrate the birth of Jesus into history. What we get in Jesus the man and the Messiah is the essence of God. God has broken through into a battered and shattered world in the form of a human being. God has become *incarnate*, adorned in matter and fully arrayed in flesh and blood. As theologian

Walter Brueggemann says, "The agent of creation has now come as part of creation."[22]

Our hopes have been fulfilled, but not our expectations. What has become flesh and blood is different than the world expected. Jesus has surpassed expectation. He is not a one-time superhero; he is an all-time transformer of hearts and lives. This is not a warrior king or a military savior who will trample our enemies and reward us for our righteousness. This is a Messiah who saves us from ourselves. Jesus commands us to love our enemies and tells us to take our own inventory—to remove the logs and motes from our clouded eyes. Jesus is the God of both tough love and grace.

It is quite simple, really; Jesus says: "'You shall love the Lord your God with all your heart, and with all your soul, and with all your mind.' This is the greatest and first commandment. And a second is like it: 'You shall love your neighbor as yourself'" (Matthew 22:37–39). It is so simple and so difficult.

Jesus reveals to us a God of Love. It is easy to accept a simple Love gospel from a baby born in a stable. This lowly infant has no choice but to be vulnerable, powerless, and weak. What's not to love? But for a grown man to choose a path of vulnerability, powerlessness, and love is a scandal. The Good News of Jesus is only good if we really embrace its topsy-turvy plan of salvation. This salvation will turn our lives upside down and make us dizzy with God's love. Jesus asks us to join him on this pilgrimage of radical loving and to trust him with the results. He orders a new way of living and then promises: "My grace is sufficient for you, for power is made perfect in weakness" (2 Corinthians 12:9).

Weakness, vulnerability, grace, and love are a dubious résumé for a Savior. Bred in the bone of Jesus, they may be the only things sufficient and necessary to free the world, liberate the oppressed, and set the captives free. *Love came down at Christmas*[23] in the person of Jesus, and it is enough.

IN

GOOD WILL   JINGLE BELLS   PEACE ON EARTH

ED AND GREEN   CELEBRATION   CHURCH

CHRISTMAS TREE   CHOSEN ONE

ANGELS   BETHA

CHIMNEY   TO THE WORLD   FULFILLMENT

MESSIAH   INFANT LOWLY   CAROLS

LOVE   AWAY IN A MANGER   BABY   HAPPY

JESUS   EMMANUEL

PPINESS   B.

DINNER   STABL

POINTMENT   STOCKINGS

OCKING   CHRISTMAS   PRESE

KEY   BIRTH

LIGHTS   INCARNATION   FEAS

PHERDS   FAMILY   CRECHE   FOOD   G

PARTY   J

K THE   FIRST COMING   MARY   SANTA CLAUS

LLS   TINSEL   GREED

GOD   WREATHS   JOSEPH

COOKIES   THE FIRST NOE

RELATIVES   SILENT NIGHT   SAD   CAND

NELY   ORNAMENTS   BLUES   FRIENDS   MUSIC

GRATITUDE   ALLELUIA   POOR

SNOW   EGGNOG   HARK THE HERALD   STAR

TOYS   ANGELS SING   GINGERBREA

SINGING   PEOPL

Christmas
Practices
& Activities

Make your Christmas a festival of love and loving.

Many families have traditions and ways to celebrate Christmas Eve and Day with which they are perfectly happy. Others are looking for new rituals and traditions to add meaning and extend the celebration.

Christmas Eve

If you haven't had the time during Advent, read the Matthew 2 and/or Luke 2 accounts of the Christmas story out loud. Share the reading with other adults and children in your house.

On Christmas Eve, bring Mary, Joseph, and Jesus to the manger. On Christmas day, move the shepherds to the scene.

Go to a Christmas Eve church service.

Even if you do not belong to a church or usually attend one, find one whose music is lovely or where the preaching is great or the decorations are spectacular. Christmas is about *Emmanuel*—God with *us*; it's not just about me. Find some other people with whom to share the celebration.

"De-purple"

the house. The waiting is over; Advent is finished. The time of reflection has turned to a time of partying and celebration. Change the purple lights to white or Christmas colors.

Change the purple candles

in the Advent wreath to white. The light of Christ has come into the world. The white candles let us know this.

Hang your finished Advent drawings

and calendars on a wall.

Christmas Day

Read the Luke 2:1–20 version of the Christmas story. Read the story before opening the gifts. Remember we are waiting for the coming of the Christ child, not just for opening a bunch of presents. A few more minutes of Advent waiting puts the focus on Jesus. Provide a plate of healthy snacks for hungry waiters. Luke 2:1–20 is also a good bedtime story for Christmas night.

Avoid a package-opening rampage. Open gifts one at a time. Each person takes a turn and opens one gift while others watch. Let small children be the package deliverers.

Read the Luke 2 story from the King James Bible. "Swaddle" small children in a blanket and hold them in your lap. Ask them how it feels. Teach them how to swaddle their dolls and stuffed animals.

Bring out the kings and camels and start them on their journey to see Jesus.

Give each person in the family an envelope containing the same amount of money—$10, $20, or whatever amount you choose. This money is for giving away—small amounts at a time or all at once. Explore the many needs of your town. Help children to **learn about giving** money to worthwhile organizations or to others in need. Talk about other ways you can help people besides giving them money.

If you spend the holidays in a hotel or a place without a crèche, **bring Mary, Joseph, and Jesus along.** Set them on the desk or dresser of your bedroom away from home. Since Mary, Joseph, and Jesus are about to embark on a long journey anyway, they will not be unfamiliar with travel.

Consider **spreading your gift-giving throughout the twelve days of Christmas.** Receiving a pile of gifts on a single day can be overwhelming. It's hard to *see* or appreciate an individual gift when it is one of many.

The Rest of the Twelve Days of Christmas

My big interest is in "What happens after Christmas Day?" In our neighborhood half the Christmas trees are on the curb by the end of the day on December 26. Several days later, strings of lights flicker out house by house. Only a few neighbors still have trees and lights up on January 1. Someone told me, "It's considered bad luck to have your tree up still standing on New Year's Day." Oh, really? Where did that anti-Christmas piece of folk wisdom come from? Maybe the purveyors of Valentine's Day balloons, cards, and candy want the residue of Christmas out the door as soon as possible to make way for hearts and chocolate kisses. Christmas is done. Get over it. It's time to move on to the next holiday. This only makes me sad.

I want Christmas to last more than one day. This section offers some ideas for not dropping Christmas like a hot potato when the gifts are opened and the stockings emptied. Since Advent and Christmas are the pregnancy and birth of the Christian year, these pages include activities to create a few stepping-stones on the trail to Epiphany and beyond. After a month of spiritual, commercial, and artistic preparation, Sabbath time is due. Some of these ideas are "religious"; some are strictly playful and communal.

Christmas starts on December 25 and lasts through January 5. Say "Merry Christmas" to the people you meet for all of the twelve days.

Pray using a Twelve Days of Christmas calendar

template. Meditate on a Christmas word, pray for a person, offer thanksgivings, or pray words of adoration. (See the Advent calendar section in Chapter 9.)

Light the white candles

on each of the twelve days of Christmas. The daily
ritual emphasizes Christmas as a *season*. The white
candles cut through the darkness of the night and
symbolize Jesus as the light of the world.

Sabbath time, rest, and play

are important activities (or nonactivities) of
Christmas. If you have time off from work, give
yourself permission to read books, do jigsaw
puzzles, or laze on the couch. Even if you are back
to work right after Christmas Day, create some
space for family time and do-nothing time together.

Starting on Christmas Day invite the adults
and children in your house to **bring
small, simple "gifts" to
the Christ child** at the crèche on
each of the twelve days. The gifts can be found
objects from outside—a leaf, twig, feather, or
piece of holly. Children can bring small toys, a
drawing, or a love note. Bring a hard copy of a
family photo to Jesus. No matter how young or
old or how rich or poor, everyone has something
to offer to others. Although we might not have
precious gifts of frankincense, gold, and myrrh, we
can bring small symbols of our love and adoration
before Jesus. The daily offerings remind us to keep
the Twelve Days of Christmas as a special time.

Listen to and learn the songs

The Little Drummer Boy and In the Bleak Midwinter. The words of both songs talk about gifts brought to Jesus.

What gifts does Jesus bring to the world? Wrap a box with ribbon and plain light paper. Write words describing Jesus's gifts to us on the paper as you brainstorm with your family.

Write the names of everyone in your house on individual pieces of paper. Fold them and put them in a basket or bowl. On Christmas Day, everyone draws a name. For each of the next twelve days, do something nice for your person. Give a hug, carry far-flung shoes to the appropriate room or closet, do one of the person's chores, hang up a coat. . . . Practice simple kindness with a small act.

Plan something intentional to do as a family every day during Christmas. This doesn't mean you have to take a major daily expedition or really DO anything significant. Just pull out a calendar and ask for suggestions: light the candles before bedtime, eat breakfast together, sit around the tree and choose your favorite ornament of the day, let the kids fix dinner. . . . Mark the activities on the calendar so they become events and not forgotten ideas.

Call or write a note to a

different friend or relative on each of the twelve days.

Send **Christmas cards** via email or snail mail. By this date in December Christmas cards are often on sale.

Do a kind act each day

without being caught. If your anonymous act is found out, do another one.

Keep the opened gifts under the tree as a reminder that

it is still Christmas and as a reminder to say "Thank you." Write thank-you notes or emails or whatever expression of gratitude is acceptable in your house. A phone call to a distant friend or relative may be thanks enough. A gift stays under the tree until an appropriate "thank-you" has been completed.

Imagine the twelve days as stepping-stones. Each day take a new step; do something out of your comfort zone: Pray a new way, speak to a stranger in the grocery store, dance, visit a homeless shelter and find out what services are offered to its clients, or talk to someone of a different faith.

Actually learn the "Twelve Days of Christmas" song. Although it is silly, it does acknowledge and count off the twelve days of the season. With its "ten lords a-leaping," "eight maids a-milking," and "five golden rings," it is a whimsical, visual counting book for children. Late-twentieth-century rumors attributed a religious significance to the song. Each day, supposedly, taught oppressed Catholics about the faith during the Reformation. The rumor is not based on fact. But fact or not, it is a clever idea to think of each day as representing an aspect of the faith: first day = Jesus Christ; second day = Old and New

Testaments; third day = Faith, hope, and charity; fourth day = Four Gospels. . . . Not so bad for a mnemonic device.

Make up your own "Twelve Days of Christmas" based on what you did

each day. "On the first day of Christmas, this is what we did: We opened up our pre-e-sents. On the second day of Christmas, this is what we did: We took some money to the food bank." Don't worry about whether the words fit; just wiggle them in.

The feast day of St. Stephen falls on the second day

of Christmas, December 26. Stephen is remembered as a person who served the poor and widows. Stephen, a deacon in the early church, was stoned to death after preaching about Jesus Christ and being accused of blasphemy by enemies of the church. He is considered the first Christian martyr. Like Jesus, Stephen forgave his murderers as he was dying. Read his story in Acts 6:1–8:1.

Take a trip to the zoo and visit the camels. If there is a petting zoo or farm section look for the oxen, the donkeys, and the sheep. Find out why there are camels where Jesus lived.

Spend a night under the tree or near the crèche. On couches, in sleeping bags, or blankets on the floor, nestle together and have a **family sleepover.** This could be one of the "on the calendar" events for one of the twelve days.

Check out the Christmas lights and displays in your neighborhood or town. Zoos, botanical gardens, and museums often have special displays for the holiday. Many are open until January 1 or later.

January 1, New Year's Day, is also the eighth day of Christmas. On the eighth day of life Jewish boys have a circumcision ceremony, or bris. January 1 is the Circumcision of Christ and **the Feast of the Holy Name.** This is the day Joseph and Mary give Jesus his name, the name each received from an angel before his birth (see Matthew 1:21 and Luke 1:31). Jesus, or Yeshua, means "the Lord saves."

Talk about the names of people in your family. Why do they have those names? What do they mean? If you dare, talk about circumcision and what it means to take on a physical sign of being part of "a people."

Make some New Year's resolutions of the "mote and log" kind (see Luke 6:42, KJV and NRSV). What are some of the behaviors and character defects that keep you from loving or respecting other people? Keep the resolutions doable and simple, even if they are the one-day-at-a-time kind: "On January 2, I will not raise my voice to anyone." Or try what a friend of mine does: "On January 2, I will put myself on twenty-four-hour Suggestion Restriction. I will neither make suggestions nor give advice (unless requested) for a whole day."[24]

At the end of the day on January 2, notice how it felt to withhold your advice and opinions. If your life was more serene and you were more loving, repeat the behaviors again on January 3.

On New Year's Eve or Day take a month-by-month journey through the past year. Brainstorm or draw the highlights of January, February, and on through December. This is a good memory exercise, but also a way to tell your personal or family story of the year. Include a gratitude list as well as a gripe and regret list. Try this alone or with a group around the table. Note important events of the past year in your city, your country, and the world.

On January 5th, host a **Twelfth Night Party** for an evening of games and entertainment. Invite guests to bring canned goods and/or a white elephant gift—something you no longer want—for a gift exchange. Serve dinner or dessert. Bake a star cake with three coins in it. (Warn the eaters ahead of time!) Whoever finds a coin is a king or queen. Send the three Magi off to a room to don suitable regal attire. Provide fancy hats, scarves, robes, lampshades, lengths of fabric, and costume jewelry for their sartorial creations. Divide the remaining guests into groups and give them creative assignments for entertaining the kings. Ask them to sing a Christmas carol, act out "Frosty the Snowman," or write a seasonal poem. Playfulness and fun is the focus of this evening.

JESUS

KINGS SIMEON BETHLEHEM

LIGHT OF THE WORLD FRANKINCENS

EGYPT CHILD

TEMPLE SHINING FOR

GOLD

WE THREE KINGS STARS

PRESENTATION WI

EPIPHANY BAP

TWO TURTLE DOVES MANIFEST

WONDER LIGHT

SPREAD OF GOSPEL

MAGI ANNA GENTILE

HEROD

HOMAGE CANDLEMAS

WEDDING OF CANA TREASURE

WATER → INTO → WINE

A LIGHT TO ENLIGHTEN THE NATIONS

$\mathcal{E}$piphany
THE SEASON OF FAITH

Who is this king of glory?
The Lᴏʀᴅ!

—Psᴀʟᴍ 24:8

Stars and kings and journeys are the visual symbols of Epiphany. Epiphany means "shining forth." It is the season of the year when we recognize the significance of Jesus, when his identity as the Christ will begin to manifest itself beyond the boundaries of a small town in a small country. Preacher and theologian Peter Gomes once said, "This is the most important season in the church's year because this is the season in which we come to see who Jesus is, where he is to be found, and where we begin to understand what he is about."[25] The Scripture readings during Epiphany are signposts pointing to Jesus.

The first reading and indication of the magnitude of Jesus's influence is the appearance of the Magi or kings at the manger. The Magi have come from faraway, exotic lands, following a star. They go back to their non-Jewish homes with a revelation of a new and extraordinary happening in the world.

The second story tells of a wedding in Cana in Galilee. When the wine supply falls short, Jesus turns jars of water into wine. But turning the water into wine is a mere preschool miracle compared to the miracle of the wine's superior quality. Jesus's newly created wine is fine wine, far better than the first round, when the wedding guests were sober enough to judge it. What kind of person saves the best wine for last when the guests are too tipsy to care? How does this miracle foreshadow the even greater miracles and acts of transformation of Jesus's ministry?

The third revelation about Jesus happens at the River Jordan. He asks his cousin John to baptize him. As he plunges under the water, a voice from heaven says, "This is my Son, the Beloved, with whom I am well pleased" (see Matthew 3:13–17).

Anglican theologian N. T. Wright agrees with Peter Gomes. Epiphany needs higher ratings and a longer run. The church year has its faults, he suggests: "In particular, it passes far too quickly from the events of Jesus's birth and babyhood (Christmas, Epiphany, Candlemas), through a commemoration of something which took place at the start of his public career (Lent), straight to the last week of his life."[26] Witnessing the ministry of Jesus as he claims his identity as Messiah and Savior takes time. It also gives us a chance to marvel at the radical, topsy-turvy kingdom Jesus is planting. Epiphany is the season when faith in Jesus takes root and begins its journey to the far corners of the earth.

Epiphany
Practices
& Activities

On January 6 (or on the night of January 5), as an Epiphany Extremist, I remove all of the Christmas ornaments from the tree and replace them with gold stars. I started this practice about twenty years ago for several reasons. Our real Christmas tree was still beautiful and fresh. Why waste a good tree when it added color and scent and a touch of the green outdoors to our cold house in winter? The white lights on the tree were a continuation of the Nativity theme of light in the darkness. During Epiphany the light of Christ begins its movement beyond the borders of Israel. The stars and the lights are a visible symbol of the "shining forth" of the gospel. Every time I look at the tree I remember the far-flung light of Christ. The stars will stay on my Epiphany bush for another four to eight weeks.

Most people are back to work, school, and regular schedules by January 6. With the frantic holidays over, I have this extra time to let the Advent and Christmas news sink in. Epiphany is the time when the gospel gets a chance to spread and marinate in me, when I get to ponder who Jesus really is. I let those stories tumble around inside of me. I let the visual cues of stars, candles, and lights remind me how far and wide those stories have spread.

The Feast of the Epiphany—January 6

 **Read the story** of Herod and the three Wise Men in Matthew 2:1–12.

Move the Magi or kings to the crèche. They arrive to worship the Christ child, bringing their gifts of gold, frankincense, and myrrh.

 Why gold, frankincense, and myrrh? Almost everyone knows about gold, but go online to learn about the precious resins of frankincense and myrrh. Where did they come from? How were they used? What did they symbolize?

 Make paper crowns and talk about kings. What do kings and queens do? Why are they important?

The Feast of the Epiphany is sometimes called "Little Christmas." Give a little gift of light to each family member: a flashlight, a nightlight, glow-in-the dark stars for the ceiling, or a glow-in-the dark rosary.

Read T. S. Eliot's forty-three-line poem "The Journey of the Magi." One of the Magi recounts the journey to the manger and its impact many years later.

The Season of Epiphany
January 6 to February 2 or Ash Wednesday

Hang stars around the house. Most of the stars I own came from after-Christmas 50–75 percent off sales.

After January 6 pack up the crèche except for the kings and their camels. Let the kings and camels stay around for the next few weeks. Send them in different directions away from the crèche around the house. Let them be the first bearers of the Good News to faraway places beyond the borders of Israel.

Keep lighting the white candles during the season. Add a few gold ones or gold star candles.

Read the story of the wedding in Cana: John 2:1–11.

Read the stories of Jesus's baptism: Matthew 3:1–17; Mark 1:1–11; Luke 3:15–22.

Jesus was baptized in the Jordan River. Describe where you were baptized. Show pictures if you have them. Talk about the places and settings where people are baptized.

Keep outside white lights and stars up until at least February 2 or until the beginning of Lent. Tie a gold ribbon to a wreath.

Instead of Christmas cards, write Epiphany letters or send Epiphany cards. Send some good news to friends.

 Post photos on your social media sites of your lights, stars, and tree in late January. Teach others about Epiphany.

 If you are a prayer doodler, choose stars as a template for your prayers. Pray for friends with lines, dots, stars, and swirls. Sit in silence as you draw and pray and listen.

The Feast of the Presentation—February 2

 Read Luke 2:22–40. Mary and Joseph take Jesus to the temple for his presentation. Mary and Joseph present Jesus to God with a sacrifice of two turtledoves or two young pigeons. This ritual, forty days after the child's birth, was also the end of the required purification time for Mary after delivery.

 Learn the Song of Simeon, Luke 2:29–32.

Lord, now lettest thou thy servant depart in
*   peace, according to thy word:*
For mine eyes have seen thy salvation,
Which thou hast prepared before the face of all
*   people;*
A light to lighten the Gentiles, and the glory of
*   thy people Israel.* (KJV)

Many Christian liturgies use this song under the title *Nunc Dimittis*, which means "Now dismiss." Simeon, who is an old man, is now content to die as he sees the fulfillment of the messianic promises in Jesus.

Who were Simeon and Anna in the temple? See what else you can find about them.

February 2 is also called Candlemas, a day to give thanks and blessings for the candles that will be used in the household for the rest of the year. The candles are practical but also symbolic of Jesus as the "light of the world."

Many churches maintain their white and gold Epiphany decorations until Mardi Gras or Shrove Tuesday, the day before Ash Wednesday, the first day of Lent. Keep your white lights and stars up as a beacon to light the path of faith.

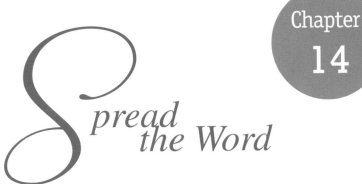

Spread the Word

I hope this book has heightened your enthusiasm for the Nativity season. If so, pass it on. Post pictures online and tweet about what you and your family are doing to celebrate the season. Share your new ideas with others and with me. Spread the word about your Nativity season practices. In doing so you also spread the Word of the wonderful gift of Jesus to a hurting world. God's Peace to you and your family.

Acknowledgments

I n my experience it takes a community to publish a book. For this book I wrote the words, doodled most of the images, and took many of the photos, but a whole cloud of people surrounded me as my support team and sometimes even my life-support system. I am grateful for the following friends, colleagues, and professionals who made up this extended community:

In the months before the manuscript was due, my husband Andy plied me with coffee at my beck and call, cooked my meals, and tolerated extended bouts of writer's and pray-er's doubt and anguish.

Phyllis Tickle, my decade-long friend and writing doula, mothered me through the process and talked me through more than one case of Imposter Syndrome.

Lynn Hunter read the manuscript in several forms, made astute comments, and offered several course corrections. I probably should have incorporated even more of her suggestions.

Susan P and the Vinton Writers' Group in Memphis made helpful suggestions for last-minute tweaking.

Connie Denninger and Cindy Overmyer gave me permission to use their lovely Advent calendars.

Merry Hunt made and gave our family the burlap Advent calendar on page 148 over three decades ago.

Nino Shipp allowed me to photograph two of her many fabulous crèche/Nativity sets—the hand-carved wooden set from Africa (pages 110, 111, 116) and the clay laughing character set (pages 118, 119, 138, 139), created by artist Barbara Hughes.

The editorial, production, marketing, and design team at Paraclete Press continues to astound with their creativity, precision, and work ethic. Special thanks go to Jon Sweeney, my friend and editor, who tolerates my endless texts and long phone calls. Robert Edmonson is a tireless production editor as well as a crackerjack grammar czar with a laser eye for any misplaced comma or subject-verb disagreement.

Many thanks to those in this widespread community who help to make me a better writer and who increase the number of wonderful people I know on the planet.

Appendix
SHORT ADVENT SCRIPTURE PASSAGES

Psalms

79:8 *Do not remember against us the iniquities of our ancestors; let your compassion come speedily to meet us, for we are brought very low.*

79:9 *Help us, O God of our salvation, for the glory of your name; deliver us, and forgive our sins, for your name's sake.*

80:2b–3 *Stir up your might, and come to save us! Restore us, O God; let your face shine, that we may be saved.*

80:4 *O LORD God of hosts, how long will you be angry with your people's prayers?*

85:10 *Steadfast love and faithfulness will meet; righteousness and peace will kiss each other.*

85:11–12 *Faithfulness will spring up from the ground, and righteousness will look down from the sky. The LORD will give what is good, and our land will yield its increase.*

119:105 *Your word is a lamp to my feet and a light to my path.*

126:4–5 *Restore our fortunes, O LORD, like the watercourses in the Negeb. May those who sow in tears reap with shouts of joy.*

126:6 *Those who go out weeping, bearing the seed for sowing, shall come home with shouts of joy, carrying their sheaves.*

131:3 *O Israel, hope in the LORD from this time on and forevermore.*

Isaiah

2:4 *He will judge between the nations and will settle disputes for many peoples. They will beat their swords into plowshares and their spears into pruning hooks. Nation will not take up sword against nation, nor will they train for war anymore.* (NIV)

2:5 *Come, descendants of Jacob, let us walk in the light of the LORD.* (NIV)

7:14 *Therefore the LORD himself will give you a sign. Look, the young woman is with child and shall bear a son, and shall name him Immanuel.*

Isaiah cont.

11:1–2 *A shoot shall come out from the stump of Jesse, and a branch shall grow out of his roots. The spirit of the Lord shall rest on him, the spirit of wisdom and understanding, the spirit of counsel and might, the spirit of knowledge and the fear of the Lord.*

11:3–4a *His delight shall be in the fear of the Lord. He shall not judge by what his eyes see, or decide by what his ears hear; but with righteousness he shall judge the poor, and decide with equity for the meek of the earth.*

11:6 *The wolf shall live with the lamb, the leopard shall lie down with the kid, the calf and the lion and the fatling together, and a little child shall lead them.*

25:1 *O Lord, you are my God; I will exalt you, I will praise your name; for you have done wonderful things, plans formed of old, faithful and sure.*

25:8 *He will swallow up death forever. Then the Lord God will wipe away the tears from all faces, and the disgrace of his people he will take away from all the earth, for the Lord has spoken.*

25:9 *It will be said on that day, Lo, this is our God; we have waited for him, so that he might save us. This is the Lord for whom we have waited; let us be glad and rejoice in his salvation.*

26:4 *Trust in the Lord forever, for in the Lord God you have an everlasting rock.*

35:1–2 *The wilderness and the dry land shall be glad, the desert shall rejoice and blossom; like the crocus it shall blossom abundantly, and rejoice with joy and singing.*

35:3–4 *Strengthen the weak hands, and make firm the feeble knees. Say to those who are of a fearful heart, "Be strong, do not fear!"*

35:5 *Then the eyes of the blind shall be opened, and the ears of the deaf unstopped.*

35:6 *Then the lame shall leap like a deer, and the tongue of the speechless sing for joy. For waters shall break forth in the wilderness, and streams in the desert.*

Isaiah cont.

35:10 *And the ransomed of the LORD shall return, and come to Zion with singing; everlasting joy shall be upon their heads; they shall obtain joy and gladness, and sorrow and sighing shall flee away.*

40:3 *A voice cries out: "In the wilderness prepare the way of the LORD, make straight in the desert a highway for our God."*

40:4–5 *Every valley shall be lifted up, and every mountain and hill be made low; the uneven ground shall become level, and the rough places a plain. Then the glory of the LORD shall be revealed, and all people shall see it together, for the mouth of the LORD has spoken.*

40:8 *The grass withers, the flower fades; but the word of our God will stand forever.*

40:9 *Get you up to a high mountain, O Zion, herald of good tidings; lift up your voice with strength, O Jerusalem, herald of good tidings, lift it up, do not fear; say to the cities of Judah, "Here is your God!"*

40:11 *He will feed his flock like a shepherd; he will gather the lambs in his arms, and carry them in his bosom, and gently lead the mother sheep.*

40:28 *Have you not known? Have you not heard? The LORD is the everlasting God, the Creator of the ends of the earth. He does not faint or grow weary; his understanding is unsearchable.*

40:31 *But those who wait for the LORD shall renew their strength, they shall mount up with wings like eagles, they shall run and not be weary, they shall walk and not faint.*

41:17 *When the poor and needy seek water, and there is none, and their tongue is parched with thirst, I the LORD will answer them, I the God of Israel will not forsake them.*

48:17 *Thus says the LORD, your Redeemer, the Holy One of Israel: I am the LORD your God, who teaches you for your own good, who leads you in the way you should go.*

54:10 *For the mountains may depart and the hills be removed, but my steadfast love shall not depart from you, and my covenant of peace shall not be removed, says the LORD, who has compassion on you.*

60:1 *Arise, shine; for your light has come, and the glory of the LORD has risen upon you.*

Isaiah cont.

60:2 *For darkness shall cover the earth, and thick darkness the peoples; but the* LORD *will arise upon you, and his glory will appear over you.*

60:3 *Nations shall come to your light, and kings to the brightness of your dawn.*

60:5 *Then you shall see and be radiant; your heart shall thrill and rejoice, because the abundance of the sea shall be brought to you, the wealth of the nations shall come to you.*

61:1 *The spirit of the Lord* GOD *is upon me, because the* LORD *has anointed me; he has sent me to bring good news to the oppressed, to bind up the brokenhearted, to proclaim liberty to the captives, and release to the prisoners.*

Jeremiah

8:18–19 *My joy is gone, grief is upon me, my heart is sick. Hark, the cry of my poor people from far and wide in the land: "Is the* LORD *not in Zion? Is her King not in her?"*

Joel

2:1 *Blow the trumpet in Zion; sound the alarm on my holy mountain! Let all the inhabitants of the land tremble, for the day of the* LORD *is coming, it is near.*

2:13b *Return to the* LORD*, your God, for he is gracious and merciful, slow to anger, and abounding in steadfast love, and relents from punishing.*

Haggai

2:6–7 *For thus says the* LORD *of hosts: Once again, in a little while, I will shake the heavens and the earth and the sea and the dry land; and I will shake all the nations, so that the treasure of all nations shall come, and I will fill this house with splendor, says the* LORD *of hosts.*

Malachi

3:1 *See, I am sending my messenger to prepare the way before me, and the Lord whom you seek will suddenly come to his temple. The messenger of the covenant in whom you delight—indeed, he is coming, says the* LORD *of hosts.*

Malachi cont.

3:2 *But who can endure the day of his coming, and who can stand when he appears? For he is like a refiner's fire and like fullers' soap.*

Matthew

3:1–2 *In those days John the Baptist appeared in the wilderness of Judea, proclaiming, "Repent, for the kingdom of heaven has come near."*

3:3 *This is the one of whom the prophet Isaiah spoke when he said, "The voice of one crying out in the wilderness: 'Prepare the way of the Lord, make his paths straight.'"*

3:11 *[John the Baptist said,] "I baptize you with water for repentance, but one who is more powerful than I is coming after me; I am not worthy to carry his sandals. He will baptize you with the Holy Spirit and fire."*

11:10 *This is the one about whom it is written, "See, I am sending my messenger ahead of you, who will prepare your way before you."*

11:11 *Truly I tell you, among those born of women no one has arisen greater than John the Baptist; yet the least in the kingdom of heaven is greater than he.*

24:44 *Therefore you also must be ready, for the Son of Man is coming at an unexpected hour.*

Mark

13:32–33 *But about that day or hour no one knows, neither the angels in heaven, nor the Son, but only the Father. Beware, keep alert; for you do not know when the time will come.*

13:37 *And what I say to you I say to all: Keep awake.*

Luke

2:10–11 *The angel said to them, "Do not be afraid; for see—I am bringing you good news of great joy for all the people: to you is born this day in the city of David a Savior, who is the Messiah, the Lord."*

2:12 *This will be a sign for you: you will find a child wrapped in bands of cloth and lying in a manger.*

John

1:1–2 *In the beginning was the Word, and the Word was with God, and the Word was God. He was in the beginning with God.*

1:3–4 *All things came into being through him, and without him not one thing came into being. What has come into being in him was life, and the life was the light of all people.*

1:5 *The light shines in the darkness, and the darkness did not overcome it.*

Romans

13:12 *The night is far gone, the day is near. Let us then lay aside the works of darkness and put on the armor of light.*

James

5:7a *Be patient, therefore, beloved, until the coming of the Lord.*

5:8 *You also must be patient. Strengthen your hearts, for the coming of the Lord is near.*

Notes

1 W. H. Auden, "For the Time Being: A Christmas Oratorio" from *Collected Poems: Auden* (New York: Vintage Books, 1991), 400.

2 Four lines of "After Annunciation" from *The Irrational Season* by Madeleine L'Engle. Copyright © 1977 by Crosswicks, Ltd. Reprinted by permission of HarperCollins Publishers.

3 Walter Brueggemann, *Advent/Christmas Proclamation 3: Aids for Interpreting the Lessons of the Church Year, Series B* (Philadelphia: Fortress Press, 1984), 9.

4 Ibid., 9.

5 Thomas G. Long, *Something is About to Happen* (Lima, OH: CSS Publishing, 1996).

6 Richard Rohr, Richard Rohr's Daily Meditation, *"The First Idea in the Mind of God" is to Materialize* (Albuquerque, NM: Center for Action and Contemplation, February 9, 2014).

7 Ibid.

8 The image pictured on page 55: Christine E. Visminas, *An Advent Icon Mural* (Pittsburgh: C.E. Visminas Company, 1984). Used with permission.

9 The image pictured on page 56: Christine E. Visminas, *A Jesse Tree Mural* (Pittsburgh: C.E. Visminas Company, 1985). Used with permission.

10 Calendar by Cindy Overmyer. All rights reserved.

11 Calendar by Connie Denninger. All rights reserved.

12 This idea came from a workshop at St. Louis Catholic Church in Pittsford, NY.

13 This idea is from Sharon Pavelda, Memphis, TN.

14 Hymnary.org, http://www.hymnary.org/. Used with permission.

15 Phil Porter, *Advent Chant*, all rights reserved. For permissions and use, contact phil@interplay.org, 510-465-2797.

16 I learned about three-sentence stories as a storytelling form from Interplay, a practice of community building and body awareness through play. Learn more about Interplay: http://www.interplay.org/.

17 Morning Prayer II, *The Book of Common Prayer* (New York: The Church Hymnal Corporation, 1979), 91–92.

18 Roy DeLeon, *Zechariah, Mary,* 2014. Roy invites people to copy and use his movement pieces without cost but with attribution to Roy DeLeon. To contact Roy: royedeleon@gmail.com.

19 I first learned about *breath prayers* from Ron DelBene's book called *The Breath of Life: A Way to Pray*. It is available as a hard copy or a downloadable version.

20 The story of Saint Nicholas is told in a delightful graphic novel by Jay Stoeckl, *Saint Nicholas and the Mouse of Myra* (Brewster, MA: Paraclete Press, 2014).

21 I learned about the simple idea of "noticing" from Interplay, a practice of community building and body awareness through play. Learn more about Interplay: http://www.interplay.org/

22 Brueggemann, 36.

23 Christina Rossetti, *Love Came Down at Christmas* (first published without a title in 1885).

24 *Suggestion Restriction* is the original phrase of Susan P. in Memphis, TN.

25 Peter J. Gomes, *Sermons: Biblical Wisdom for Daily Living* (New York: William Morrow and Company, 1998), 30–31.

26 N. T. Wright, *For All the Saints: Remembering the Christian Departed* (Harrisburg, PA: Morehouse Publishing, 2004), 57.

About Paraclete Press

Who We Are

Paraclete Press is a publisher of books, recordings, and DVDs on Christian spirituality. Our publishing represents a full expression of Christian belief and practice—from Catholic to Evangelical, from Protestant to Orthodox.

We are the publishing arm of the Community of Jesus, an ecumenical monastic community in the Benedictine tradition. As such, we are uniquely positioned in the marketplace without connection to a large corporation and with informal relationships to many branches and denominations of faith.

What We Are Doing

Paraclete Press Books Paraclete publishes books that show the richness and depth of what it means to be Christian. Although Benedictine spirituality is at the heart of all that we do, we publish books that reflect the Christian experience across many cultures, time periods, and houses of worship. We publish books that nourish the vibrant life of the church and its people—books about spiritual practice, formation, history, ideas, and customs.

We have several different series, including the best-selling Paraclete Essentials and Paraclete Giants series of classic texts in contemporary English; Voices from the Monastery—men and women monastics writing about living a spiritual life today; award-winning poetry; best-selling gift books for children on the occasions of baptism and first communion; and the Active Prayer Series that brings creativity and liveliness to any life of prayer.

Mount Tabor Books Paraclete's Mount Tabor Books series focuses on liturgical worship, art and art history, ecumenism, and the first-millennium church.

Paraclete Recordings From Gregorian chant to contemporary American choral works, our music recordings celebrate sacred choral music through the centuries. Paraclete Recordings is the record label of the internationally acclaimed choir Gloriæ Dei Cantores, praised for their "rapt and fathomless spiritual intensity" by *American Record Guide,* and the Gloriæ Dei Cantores Schola, which specializes in the study and performance of Gregorian chant. Paraclete Press is also the exclusive North American distributor of the recordings of the Monastic Choir of St. Peter's Abbey in Solesmes, France, long considered to be a leading authority on Gregorian chant.

Paraclete Video Productions Our DVDs offer spiritual help, healing, and biblical guidance for life issues: grief and loss, marriage, forgiveness, anger management, facing death, and spiritual formation.

Learn more about us at our website:
www.paracletepress.com
or phone us toll-free at 1.800.451.5006

SCAN
TO
READ
MORE

Sybil MacBeth created *Praying in Color* . . .

Praying in Color
Drawing a New Path to God
Sybil MacBeth
ISBN: 978-1-55725-512-9 | $17.99, Paperback

Maybe you hunger to know God better. Maybe you love color. Maybe you are a visual learner, a distractible soul, or a word-weary pray-er. Perhaps you struggle with a short attention span or a restless body. This new prayer form can take as little or as much time as you have, from 15 minutes to a weekend retreat. "A new prayer form gives God a new door to penetrate the locked cells of our hearts and minds," explains Sybil MacBeth.

Praying in Color Journal
Sybil MacBeth
ISBN: 978-1-55725-618-8 | $16.99, Paperback

Thousands of people have already discovered this truly simple, transformative spiritual practice. This companion to the surprise bestseller *Praying in Color* provides the perfect journal to help you experience a whole new way of talking with God—by "praying in color."

Praying in Color
Drawing a New Path to God (Portable Edition)
Sybil MacBeth
ISBN: 978-1-61261-353-6 | $14.99, Paperback

This smaller, "portable" edition of the bestseller *Praying in Color* has been revised and updated by the author for this new format.

Praying in Color—*Kids' Edition*
Sybil MacBeth
ISBN: 978-1-55725-595-2 | $16.99, Paperback

Now kids can pray in color, too! This first-of-its-kind resource will forever change the way kids pray—and how adults try to teach them to do it. This is prayer that makes sense to kids. Drawing with markers or crayons is half the prayer; the other half is carrying the visual memories throughout the day.

Available from most booksellers or through Paraclete Press:
www.paracletepress.com | 1-800-451-5006
Try your local bookstore first.